MANGA

THE MONSTER BOOK OF MANGA

CREATURES AND CHARACTERS
COLORING BOOK

T0017934

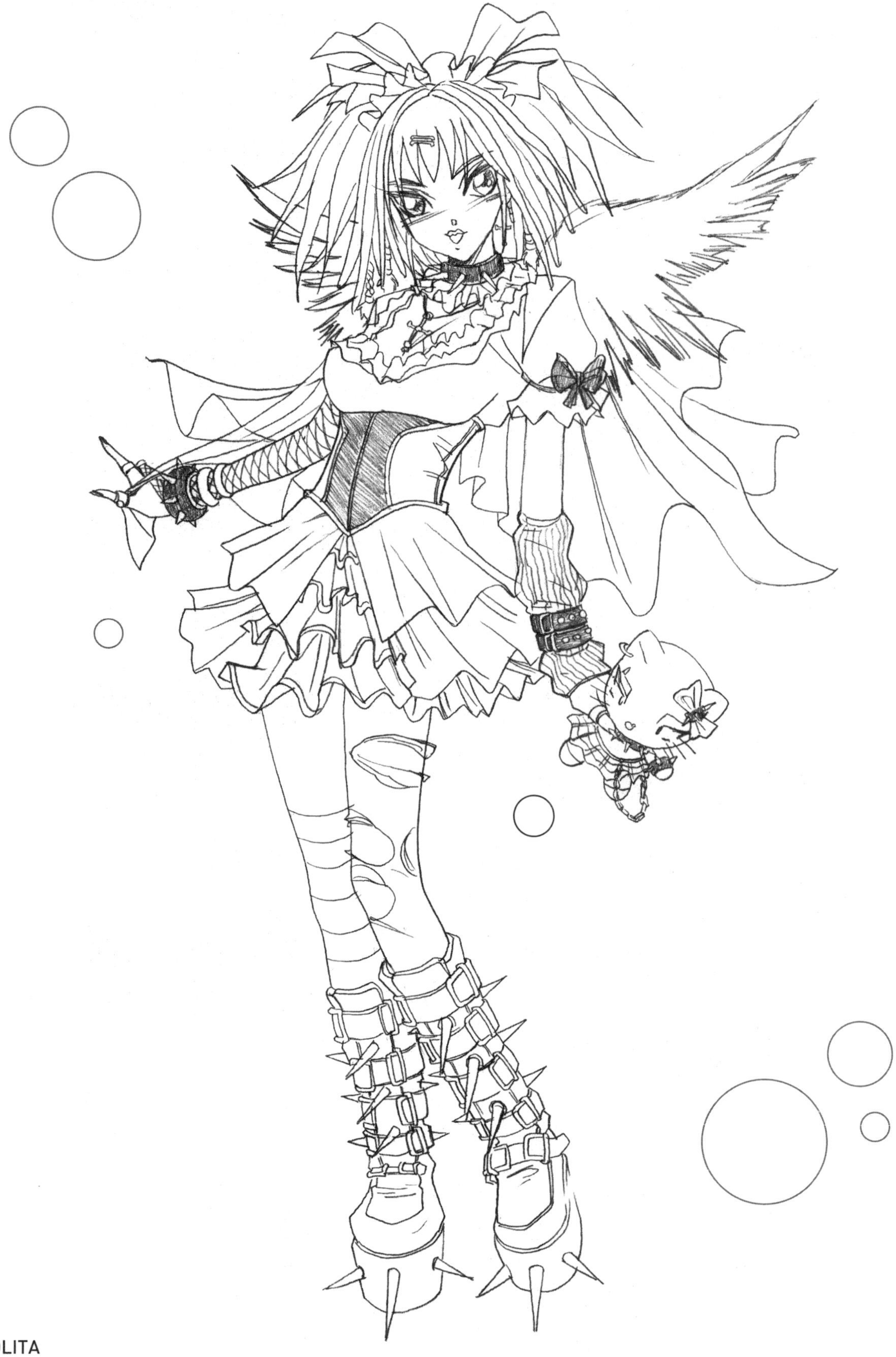

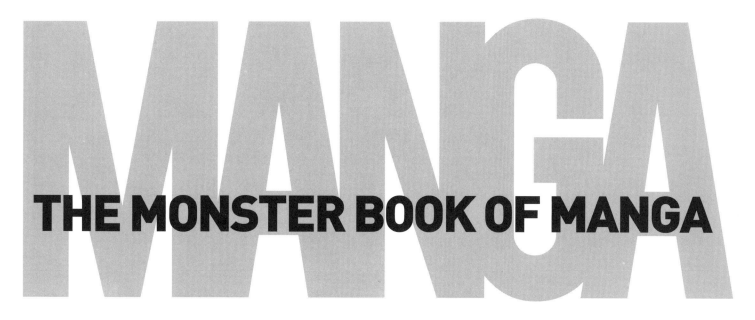

THE MONSTER BOOK OF MANGA

CREATURES AND CHARACTERS
COLORING BOOK

ESTUDIO JOSO AND IKARI STUDIO

HARPER
DESIGN

An Imprint of HarperCollinsPublishers

TABLE OF CONTENTS

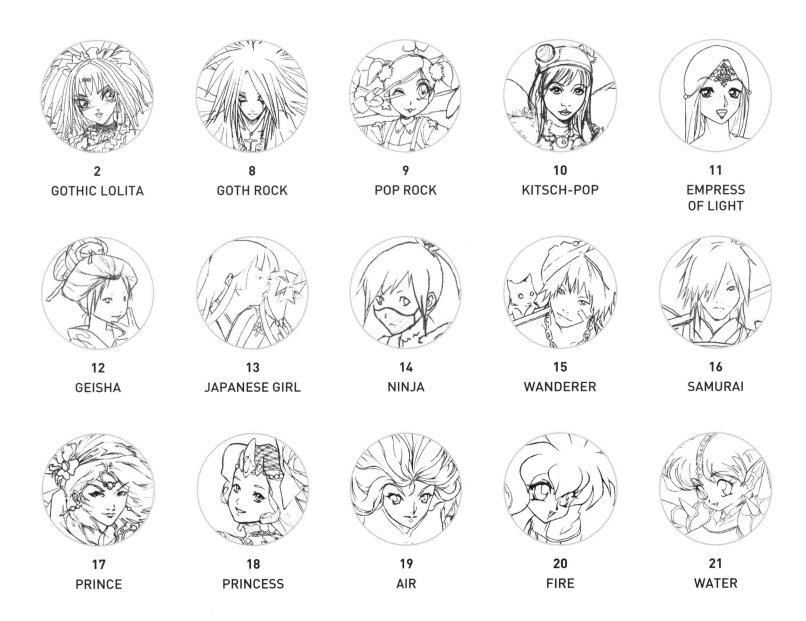

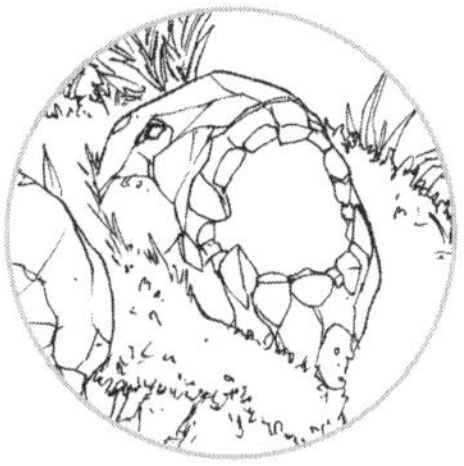
22
EARTH

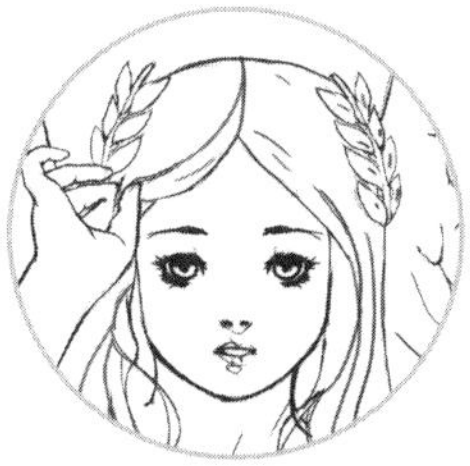
23
ANGEL

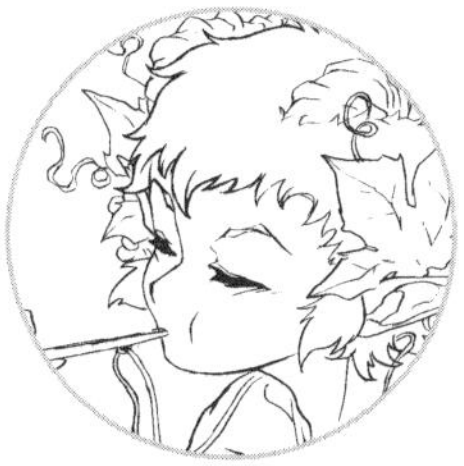
24
FAUN

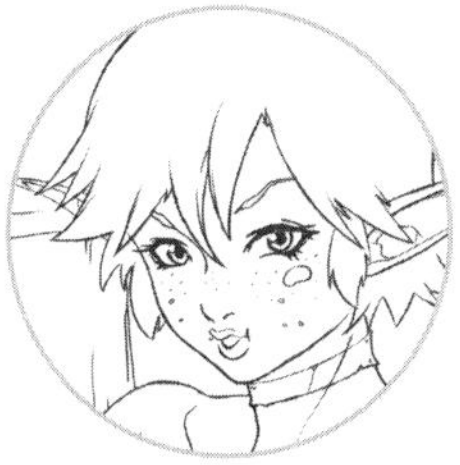
25
PIXIE

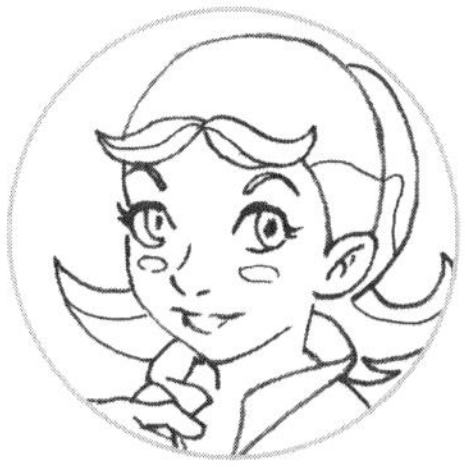
26
PARA PARA DANCER

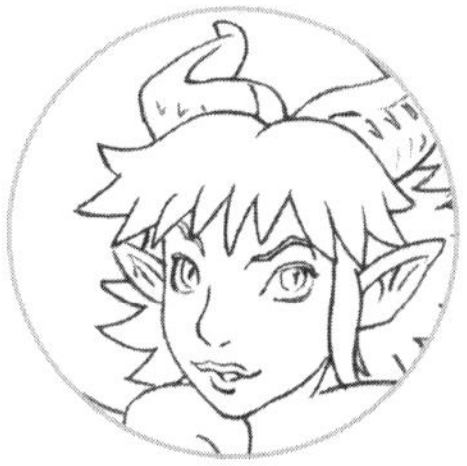
27
SUCCUBUS

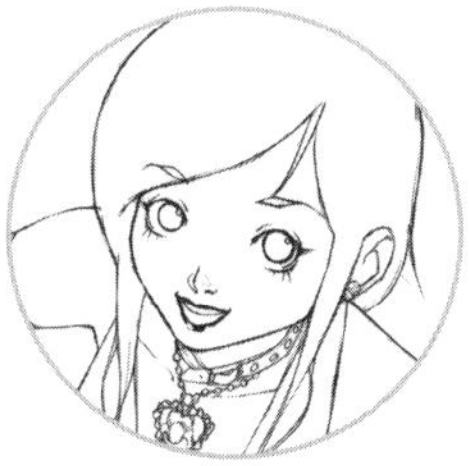
28
SORCERESS

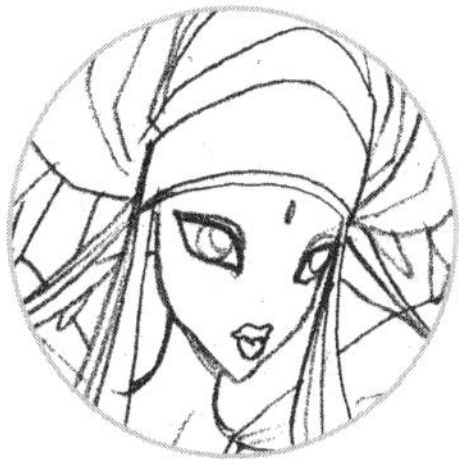
29
PRINCESS NEBULA

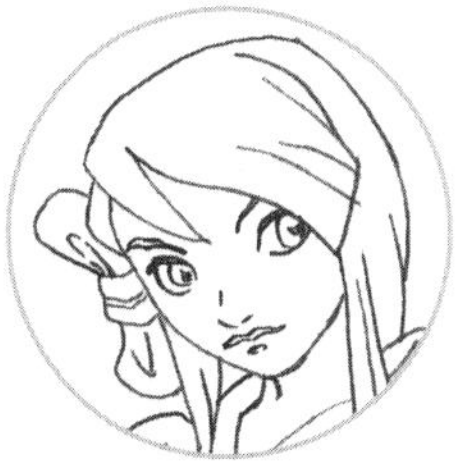
30
TRADITIONAL DANCER

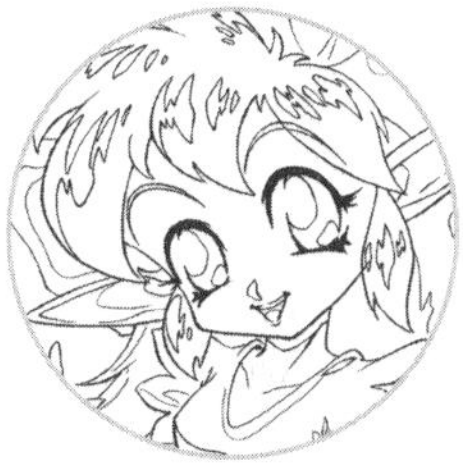
31
FEMALE ELF

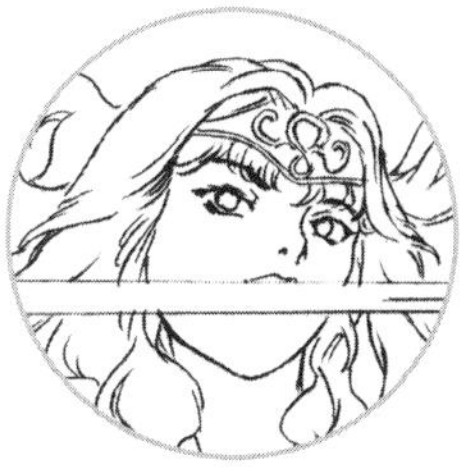
32
THE LADY OF THE LAKE

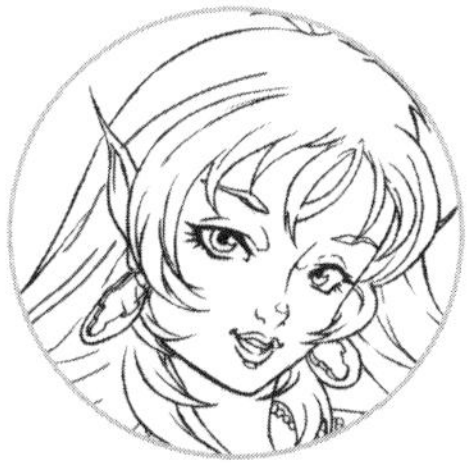
33
SIREN

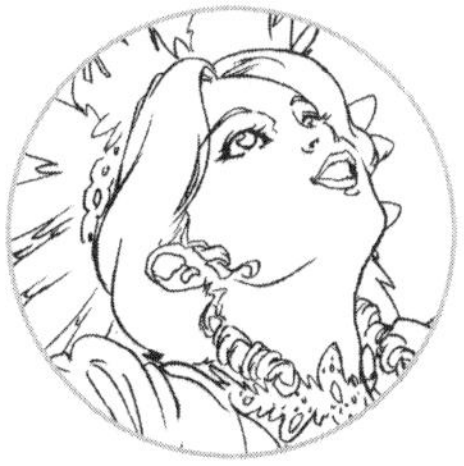
34
SWAN LADY

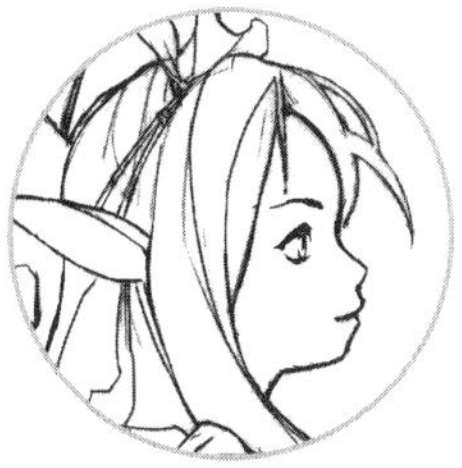
35
YOUNG FAIRY

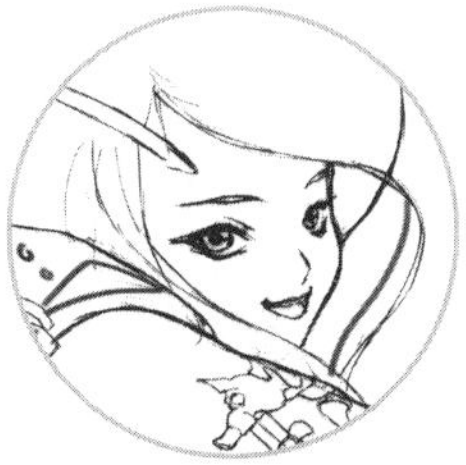
36
WATER NYMPH

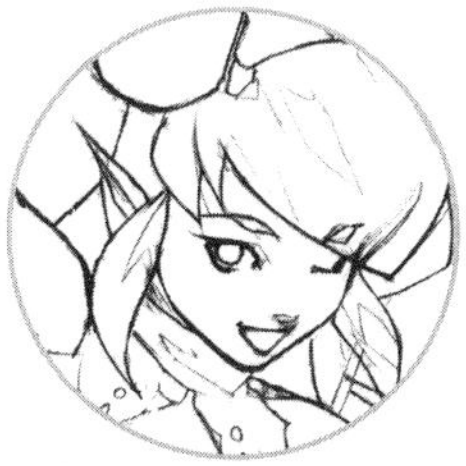
37
FAIRIES

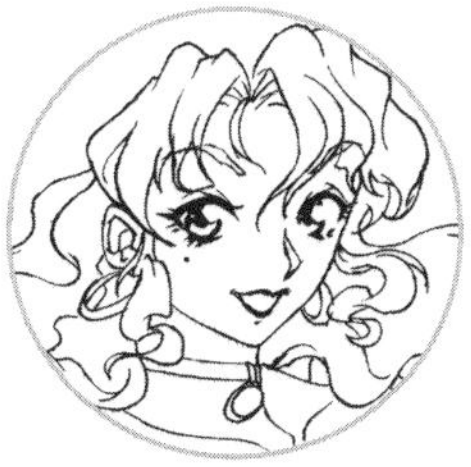
38
FOREST WITCHES

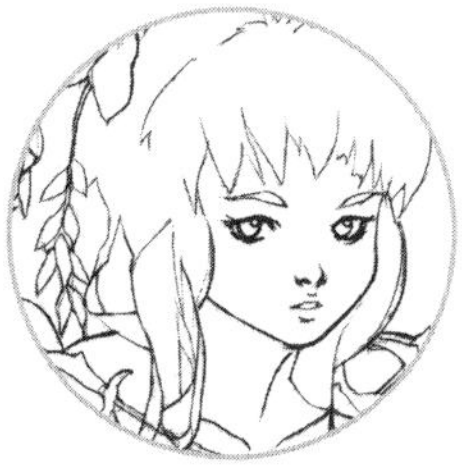
39
EARTH LADY

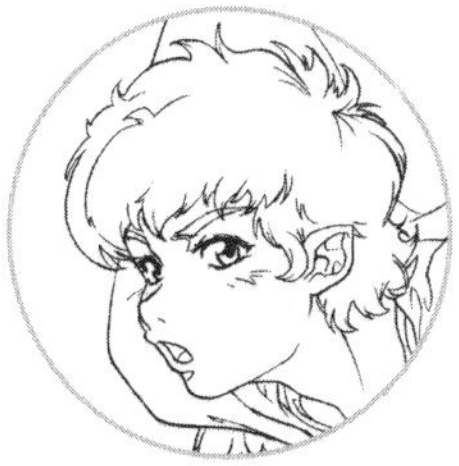
40
HALFLING

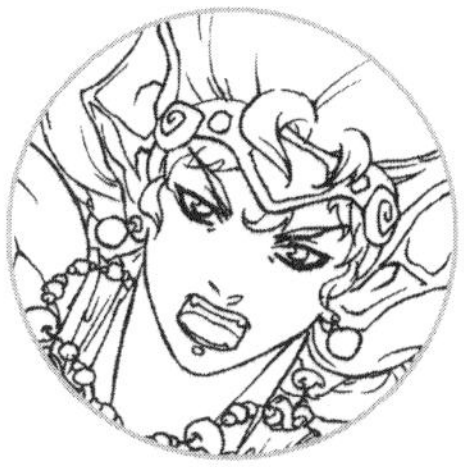
41
THE WINGED

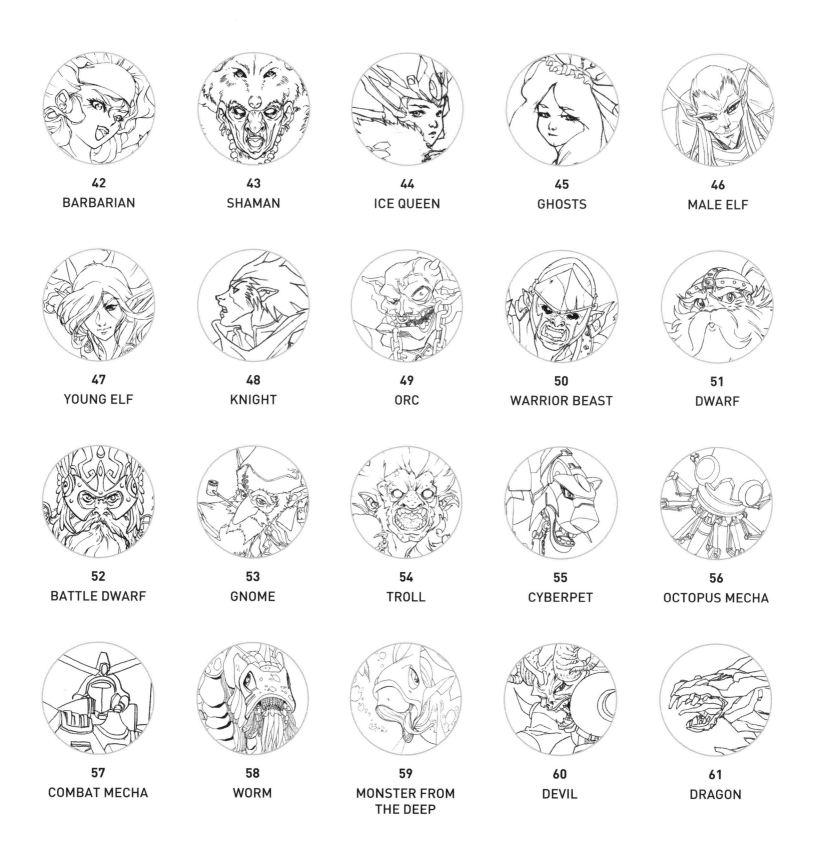

42 BARBARIAN

43 SHAMAN

44 ICE QUEEN

45 GHOSTS

46 MALE ELF

47 YOUNG ELF

48 KNIGHT

49 ORC

50 WARRIOR BEAST

51 DWARF

52 BATTLE DWARF

53 GNOME

54 TROLL

55 CYBERPET

56 OCTOPUS MECHA

57 COMBAT MECHA

58 WORM

59 MONSTER FROM THE DEEP

60 DEVIL

61 DRAGON

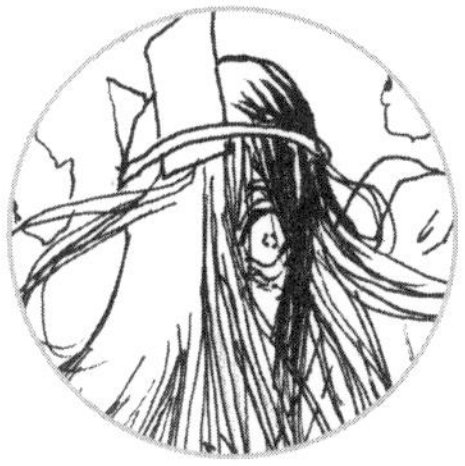

62
TENTACLE MONSTER

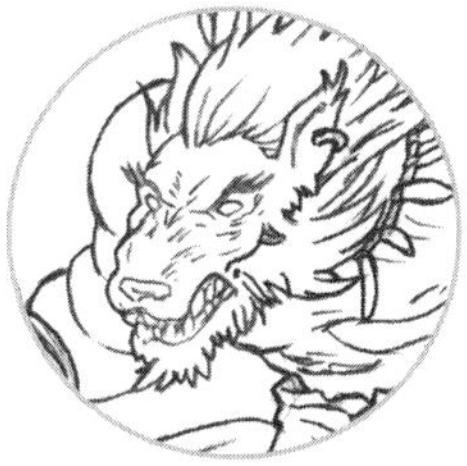

63
WEREWOLF

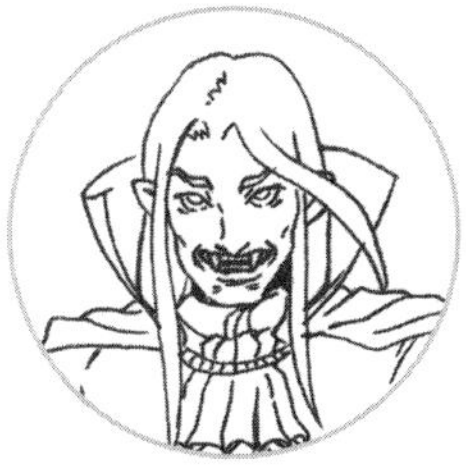

64
VAMPIRE

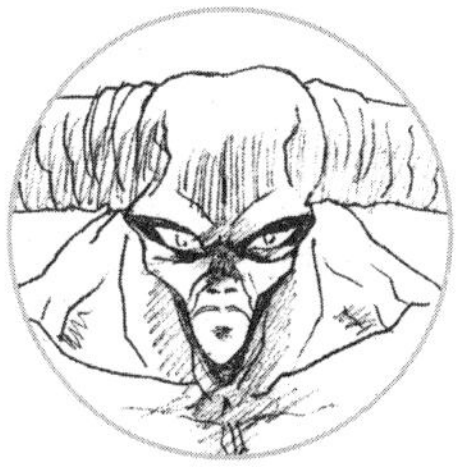

65
DEMON

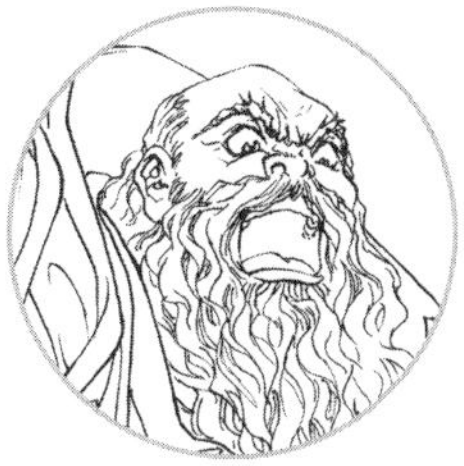

66
MASTER OF TIME

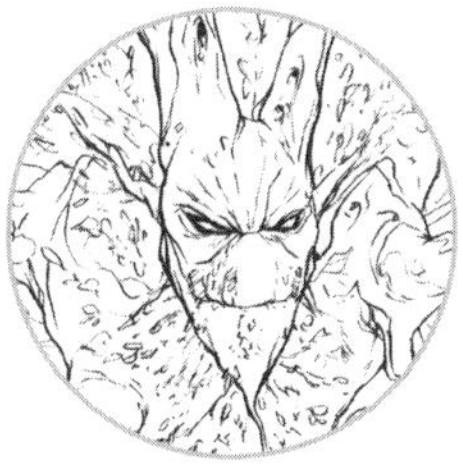

67
TREE MAN

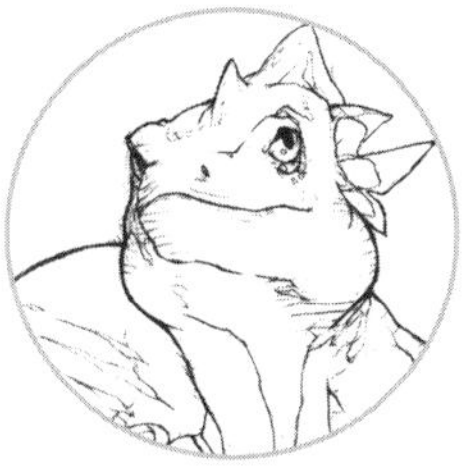

68
LIZARD MEN

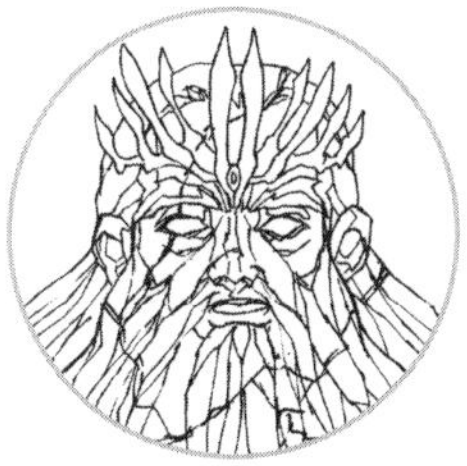

69
STONE ORACLE

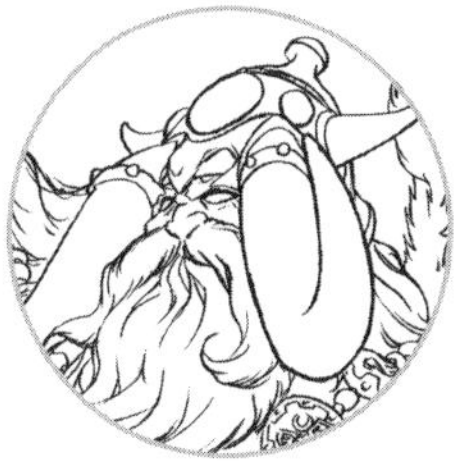

70
ICE GIANT

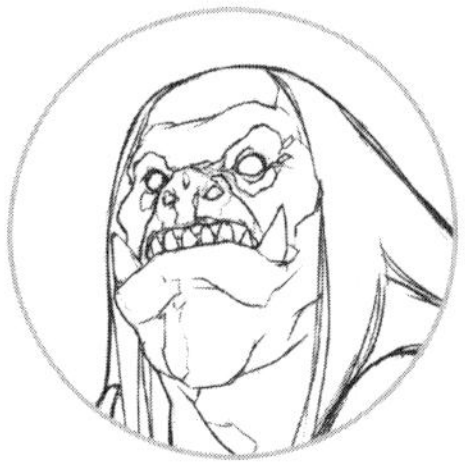

71
MAN BEAST

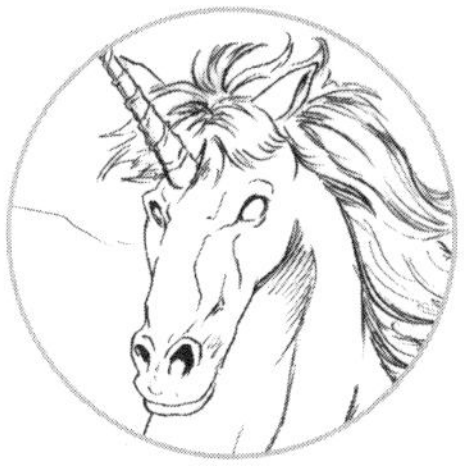

72
UNICORN

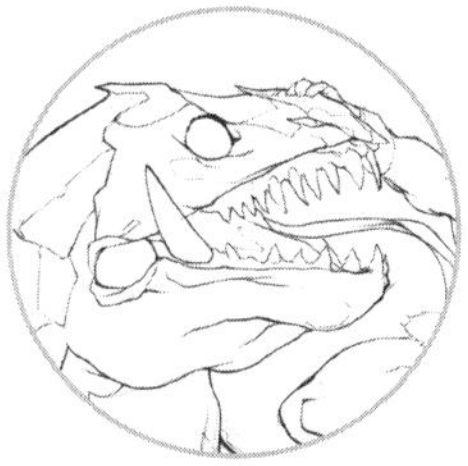

73
LAKE MONSTER

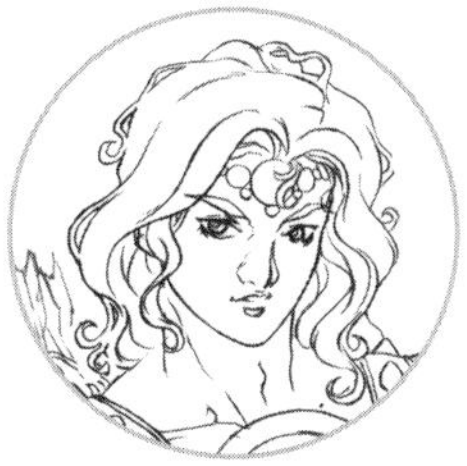

74
CENTAUR

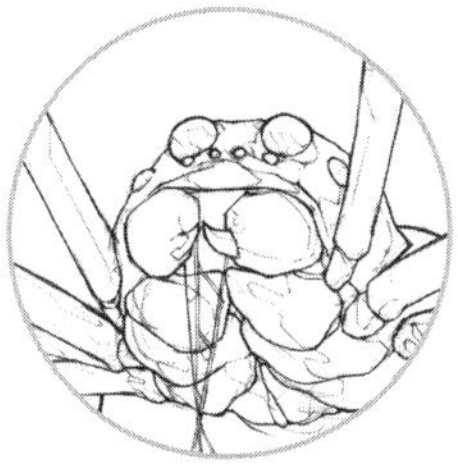

75
GIANT SPIDER

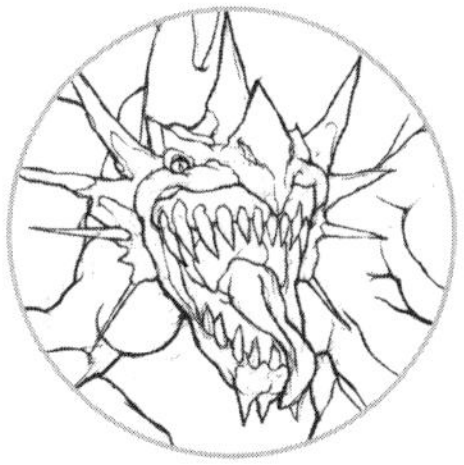

76
FLYING DRAGON

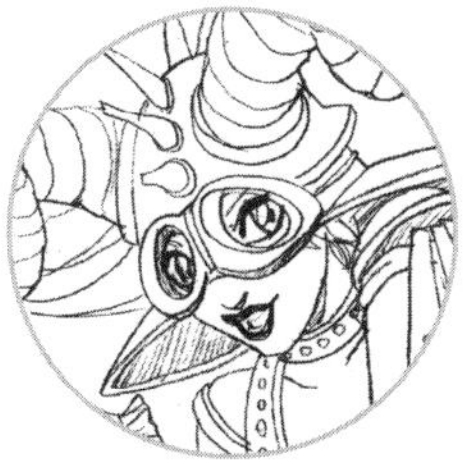

77
AMAZON

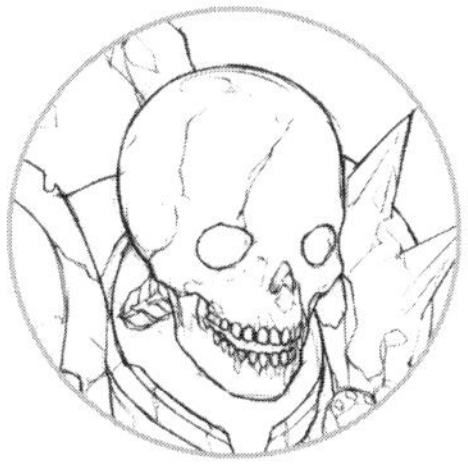

78
SKELETON

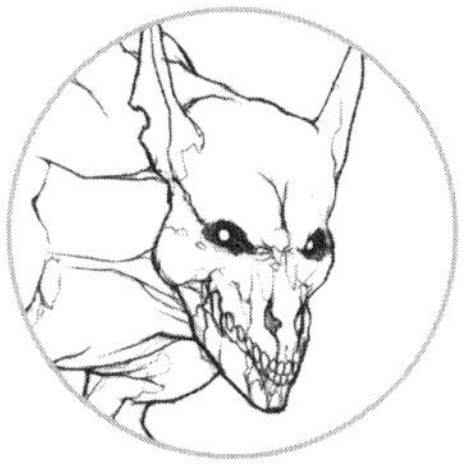

79
HOUND OF HELL

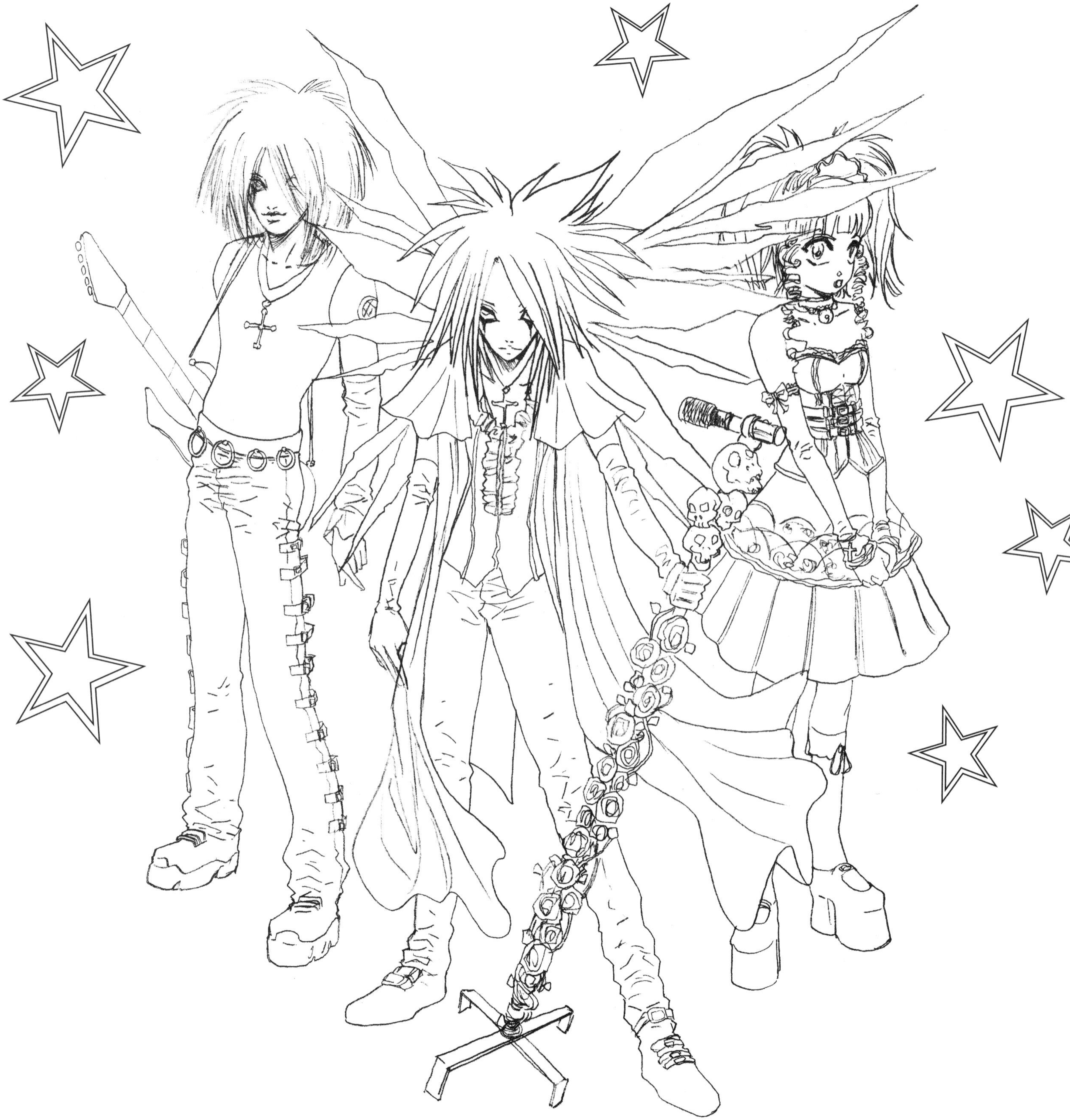

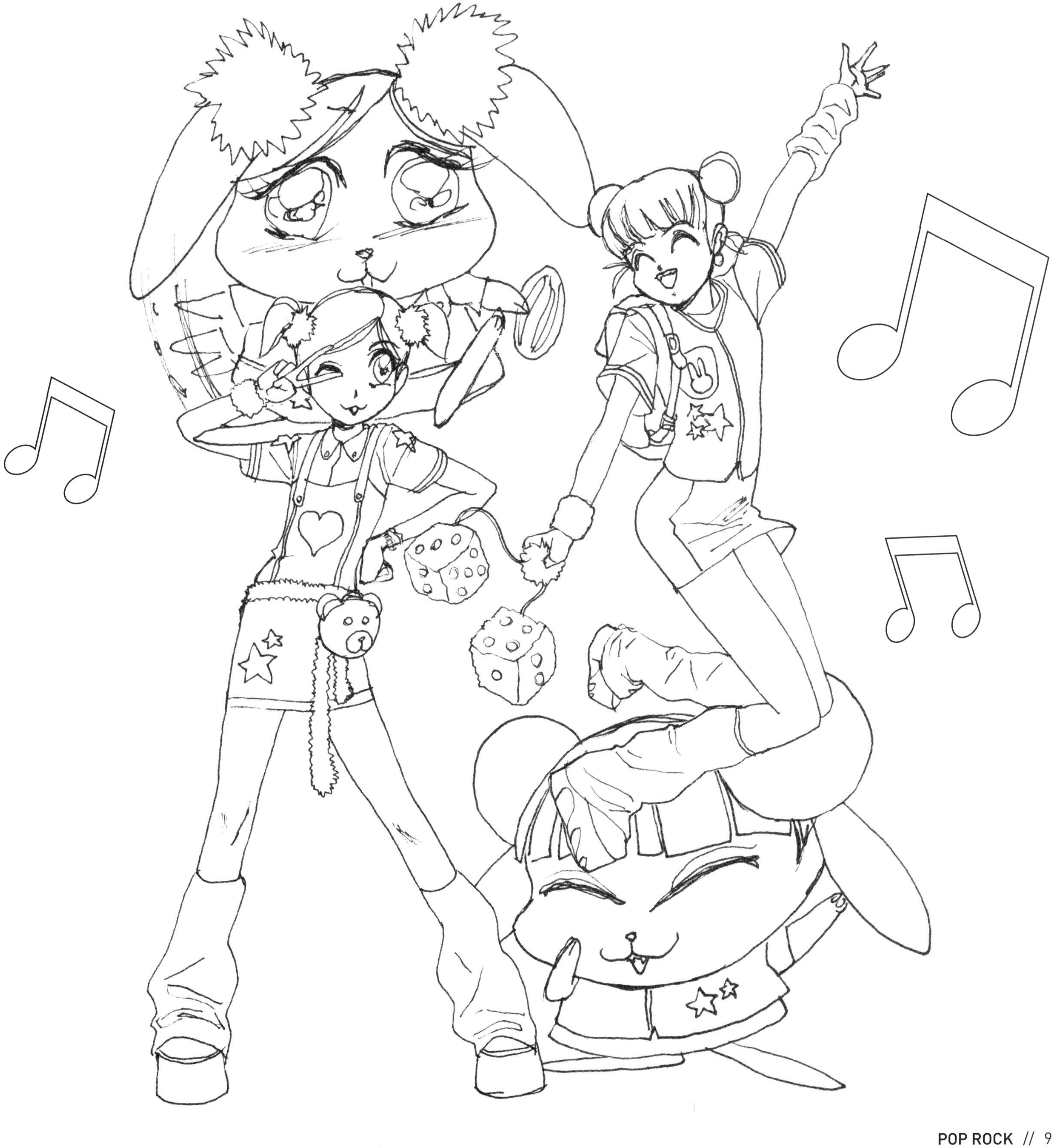

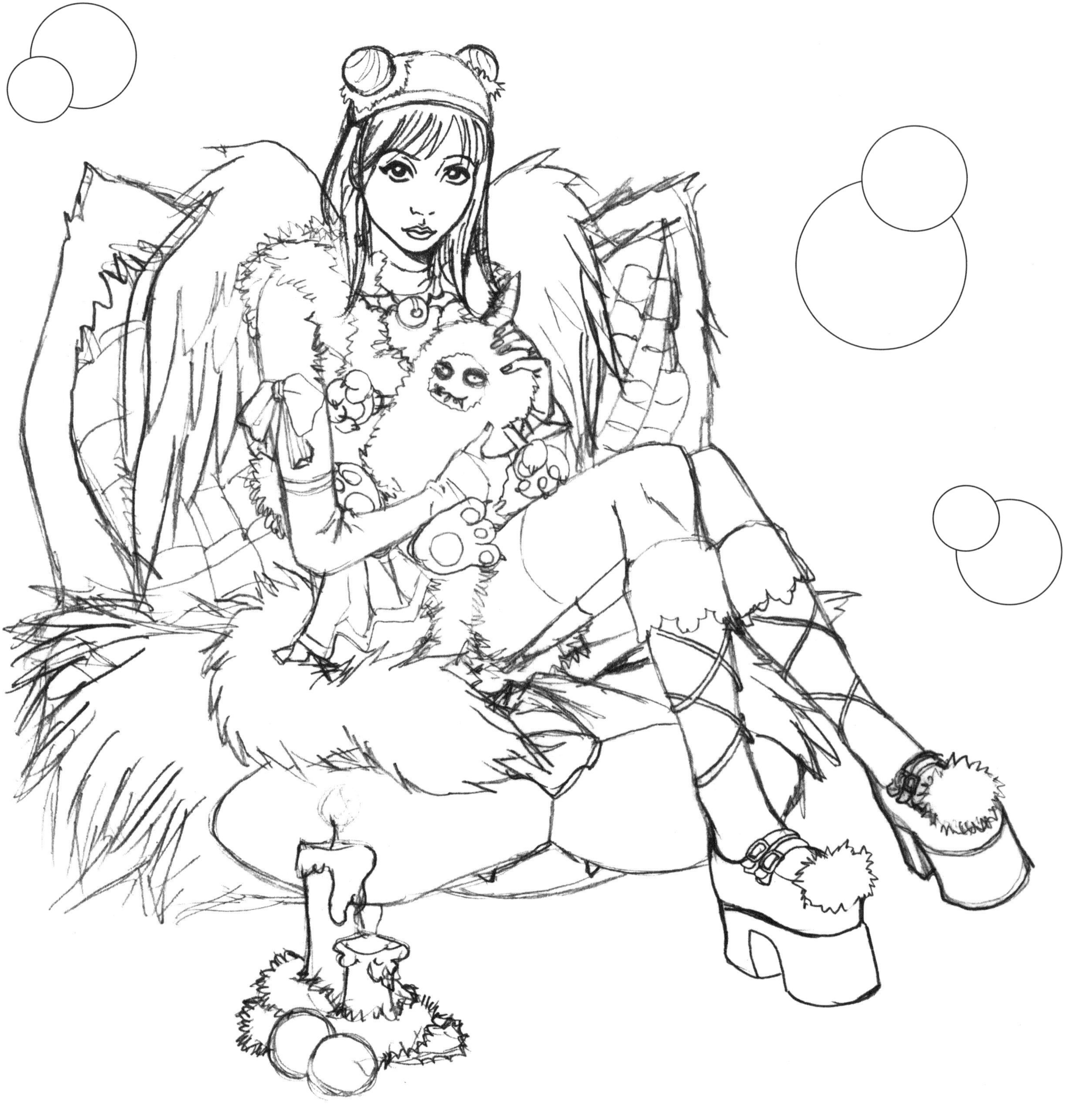

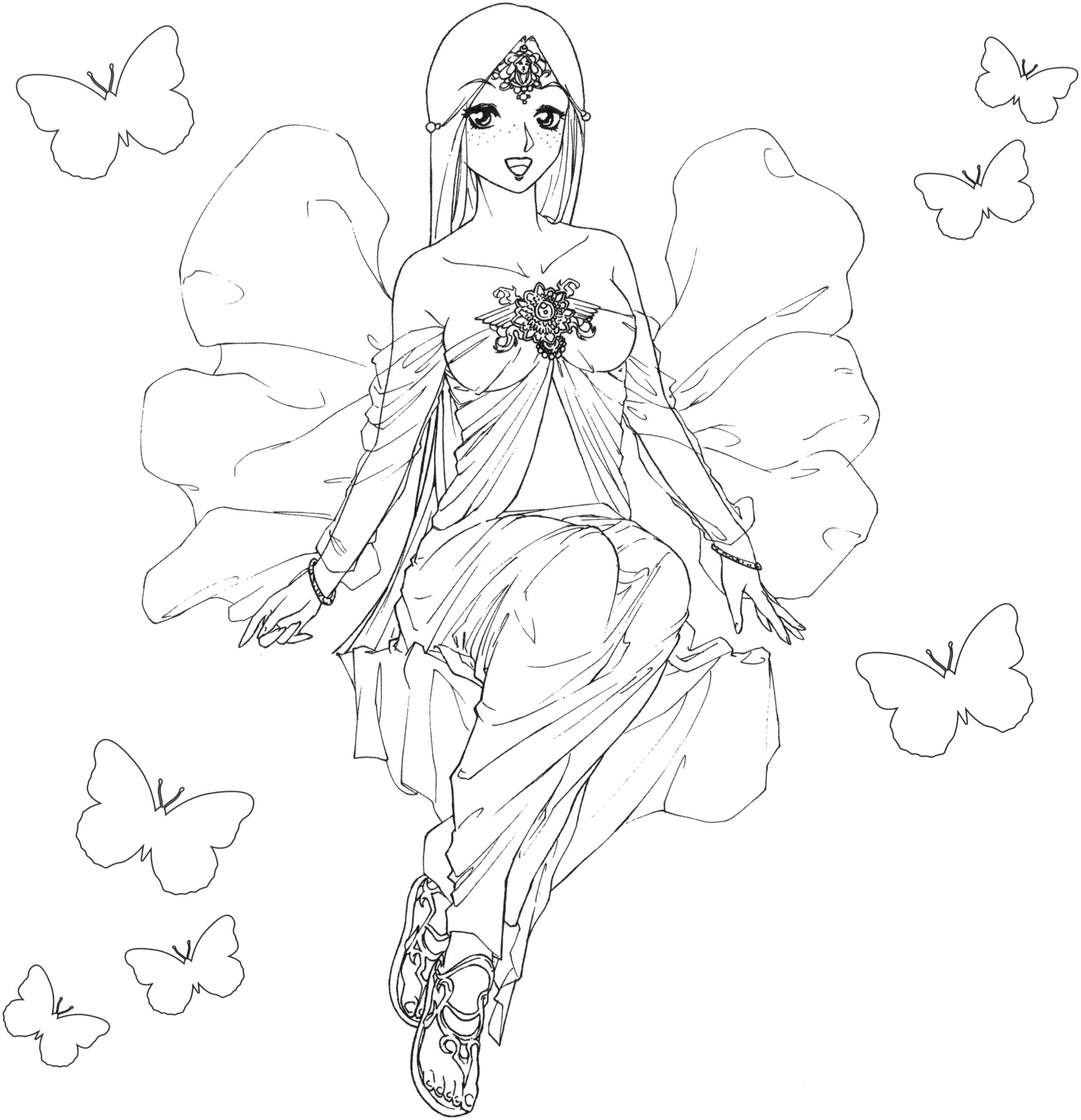

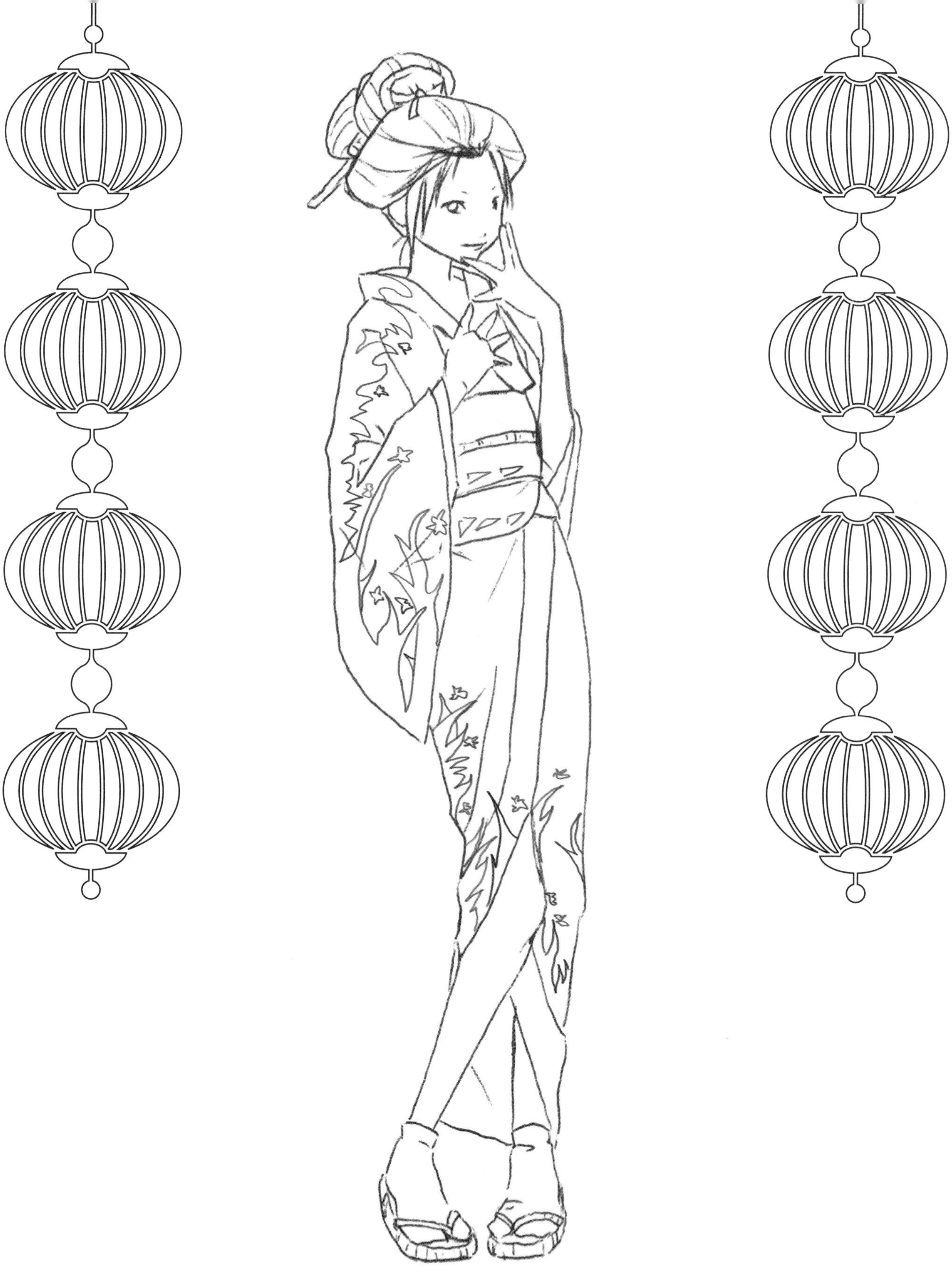

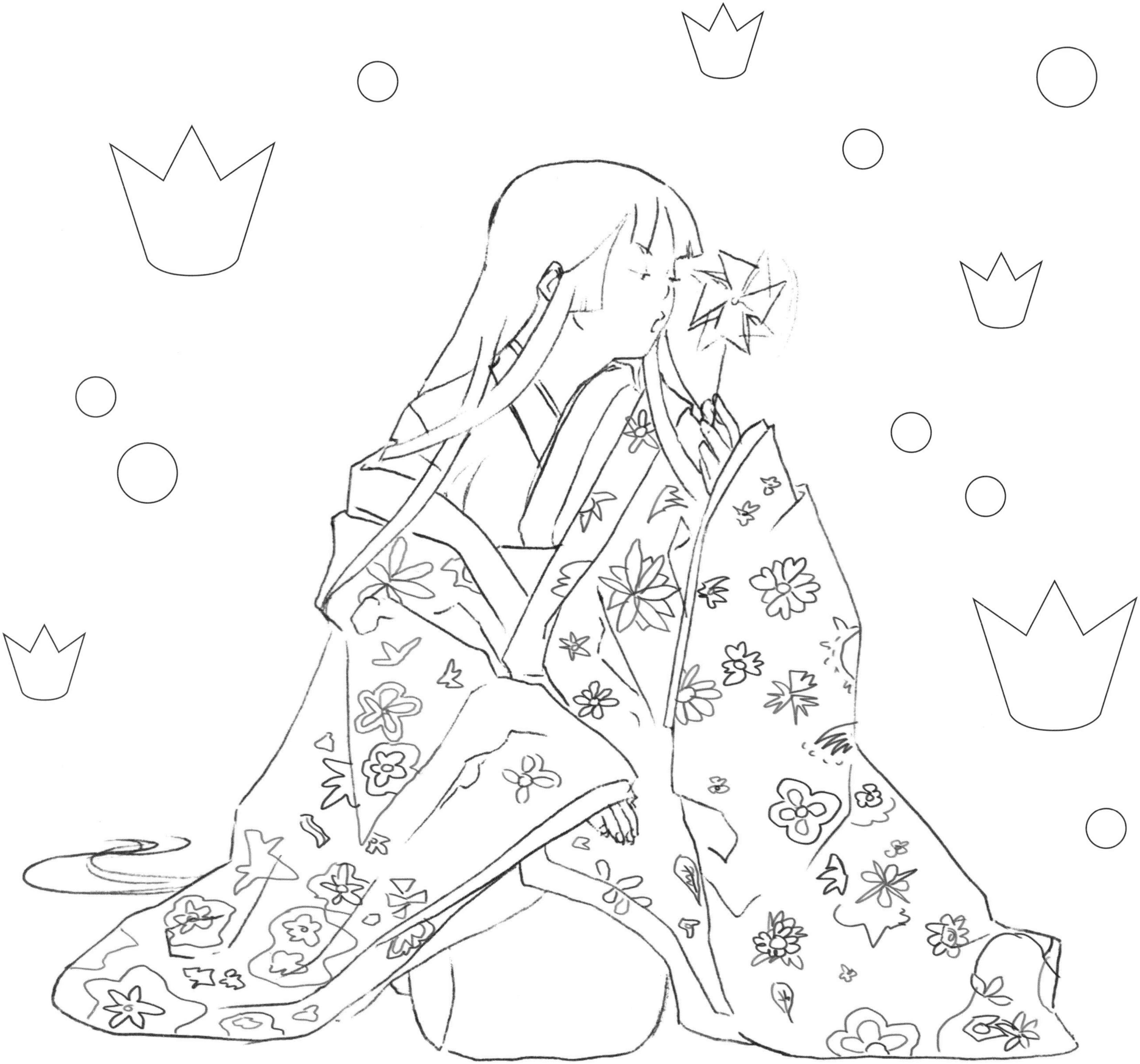

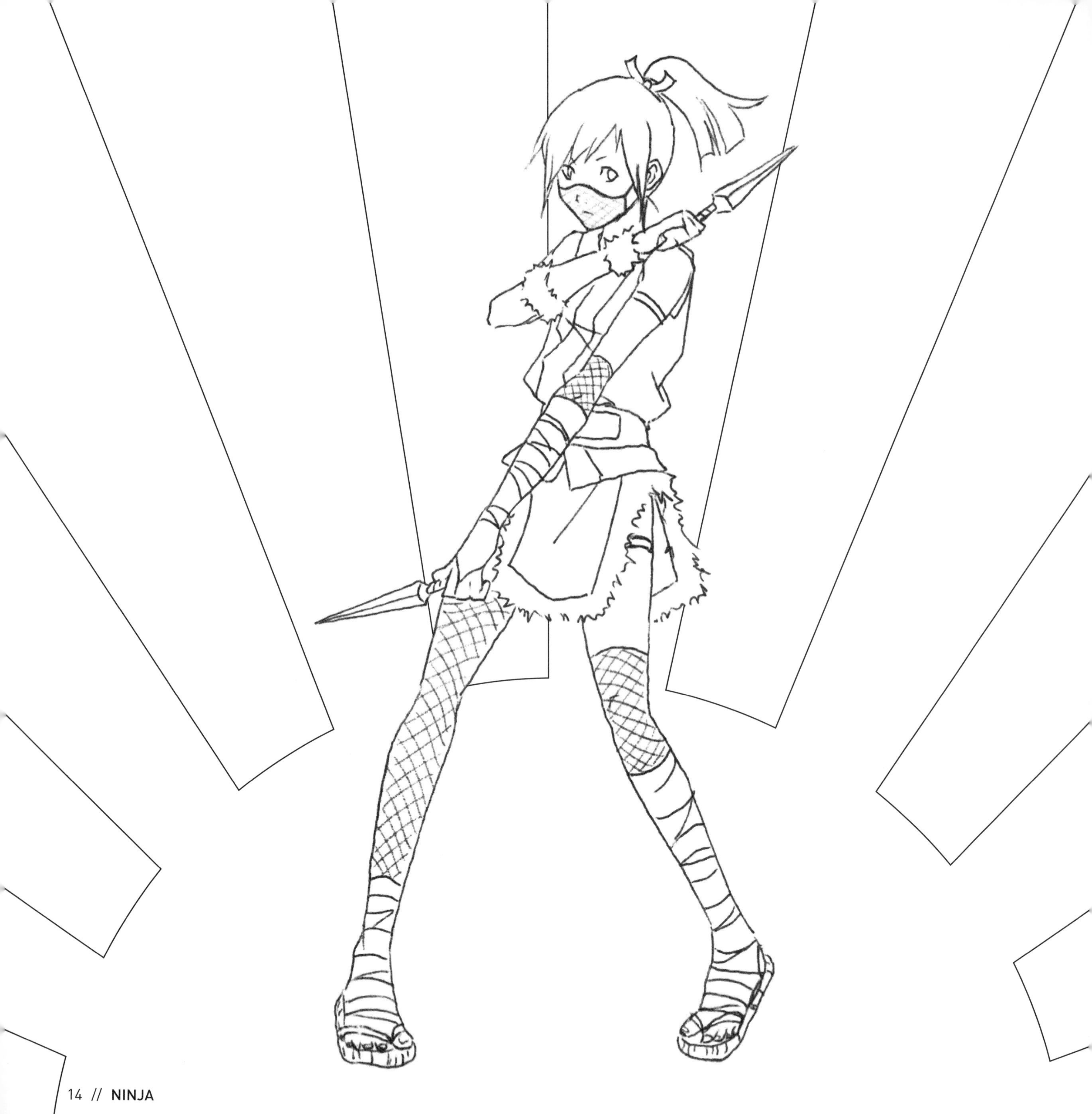

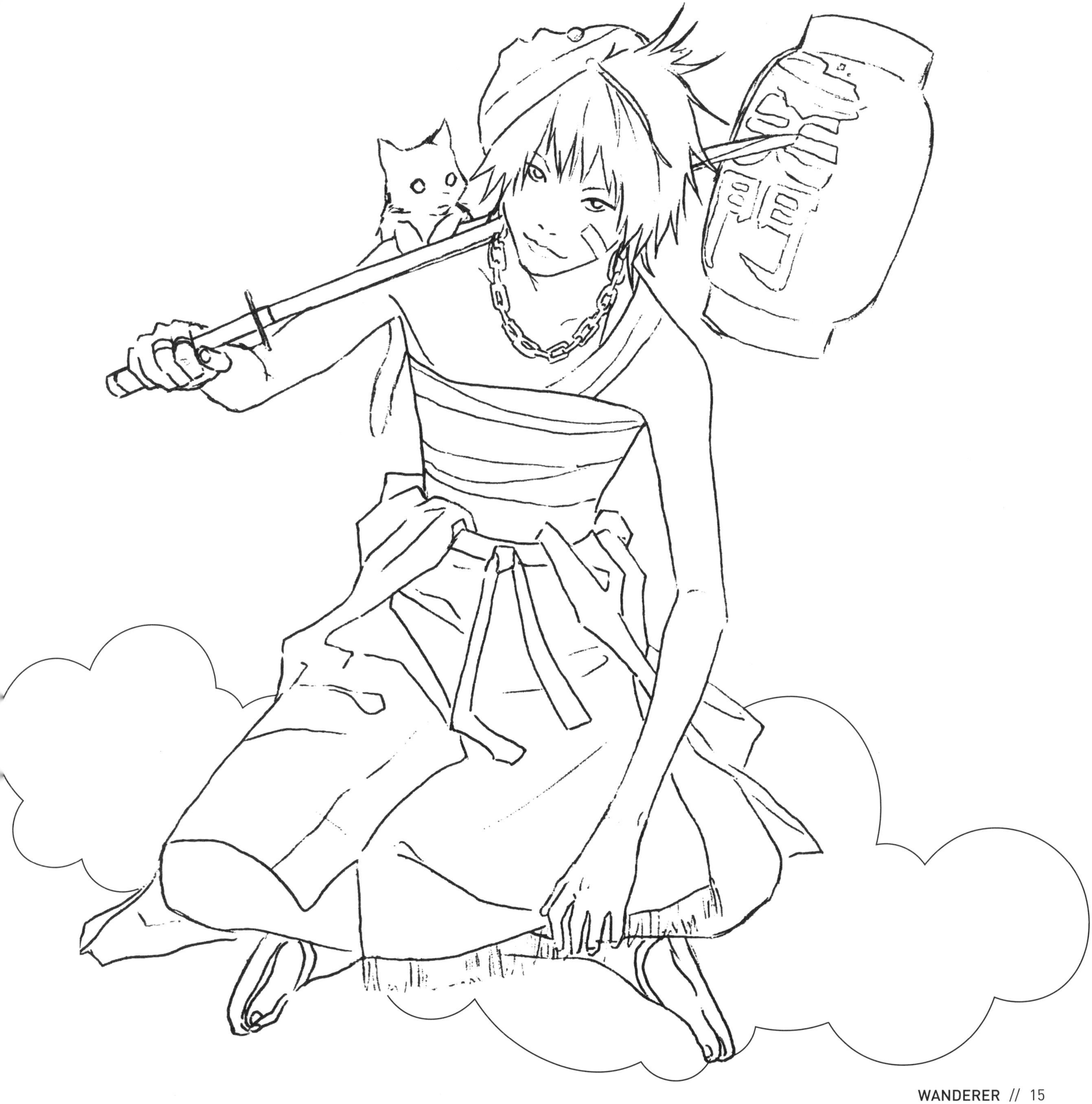

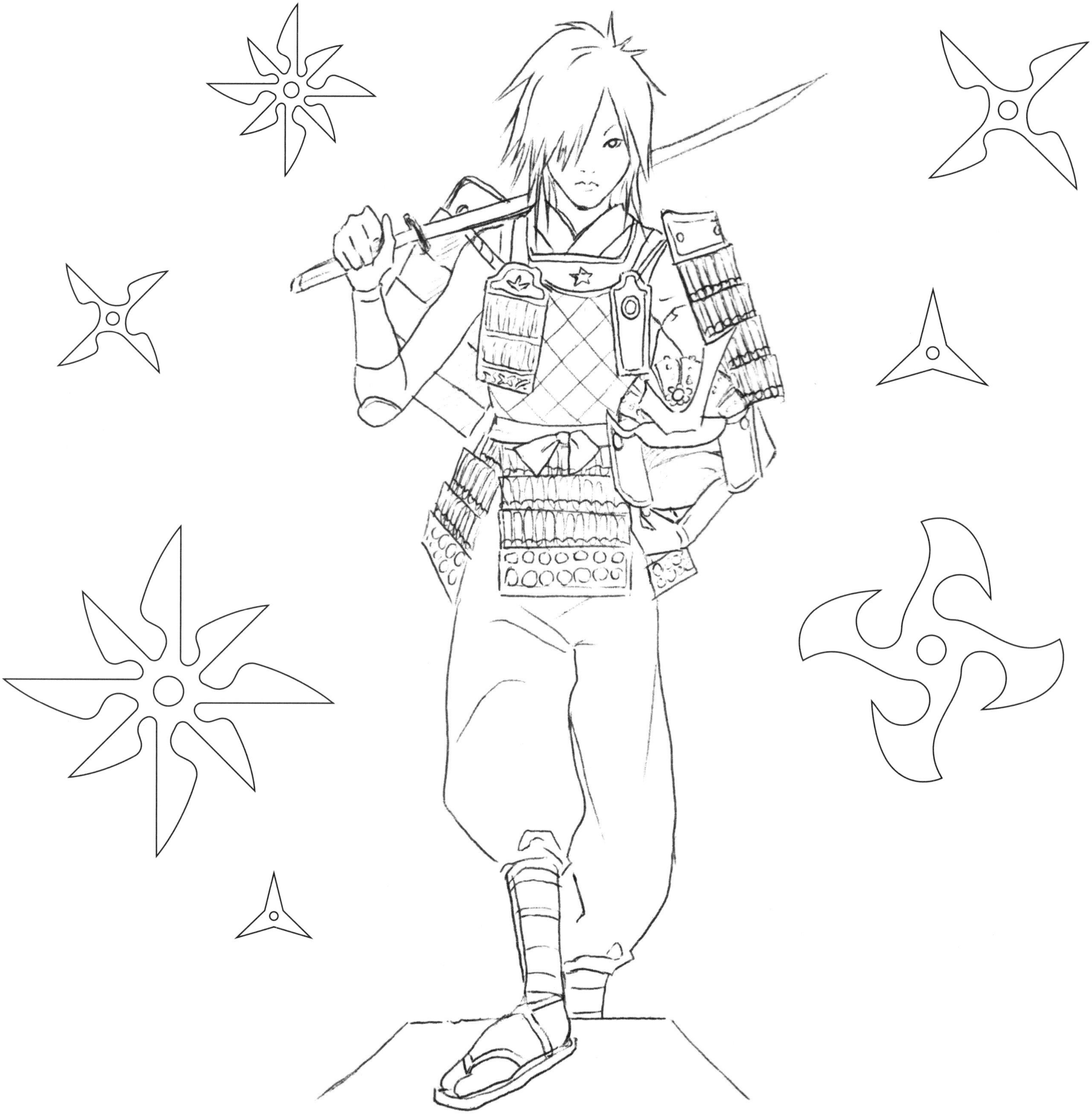

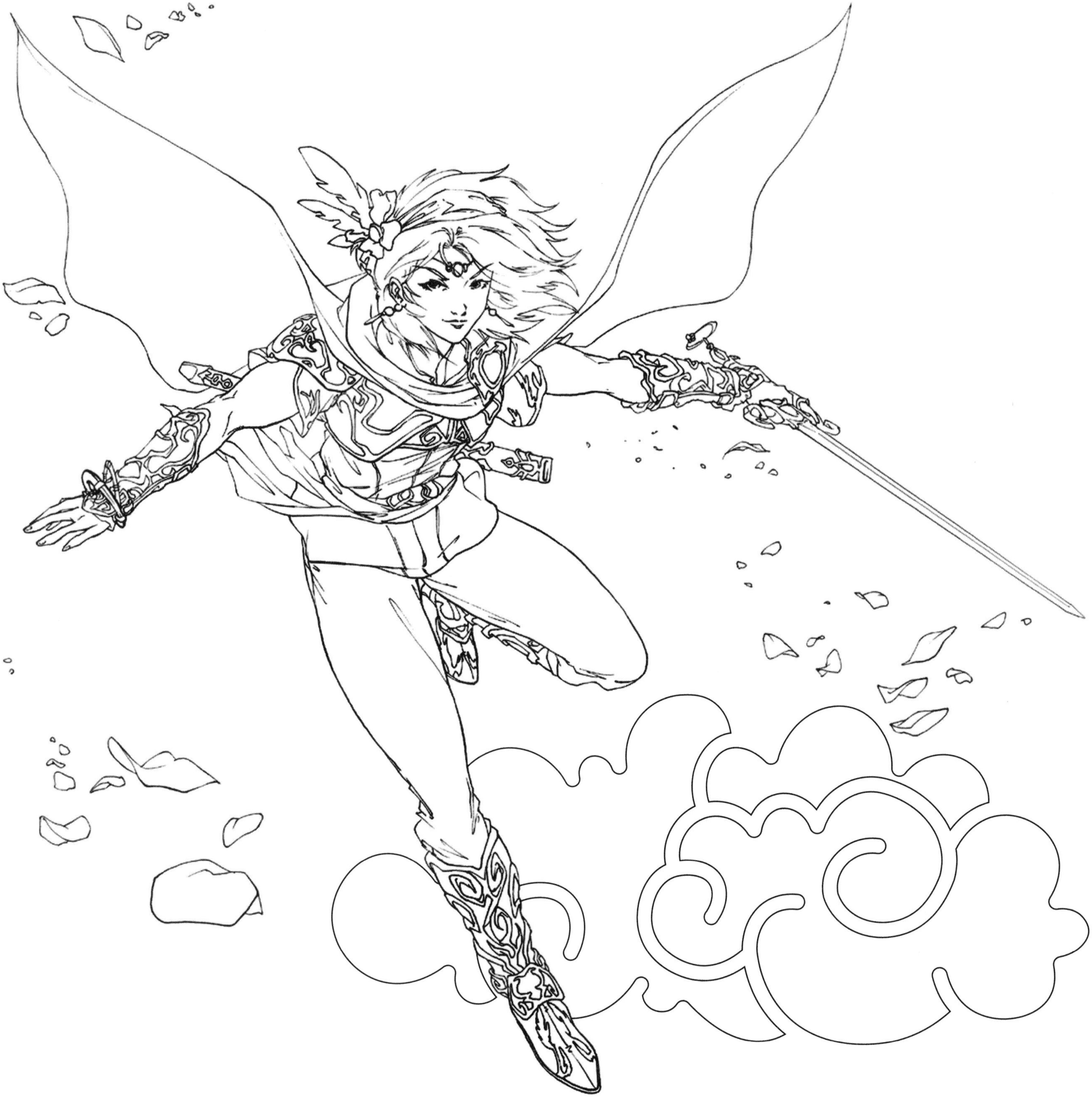

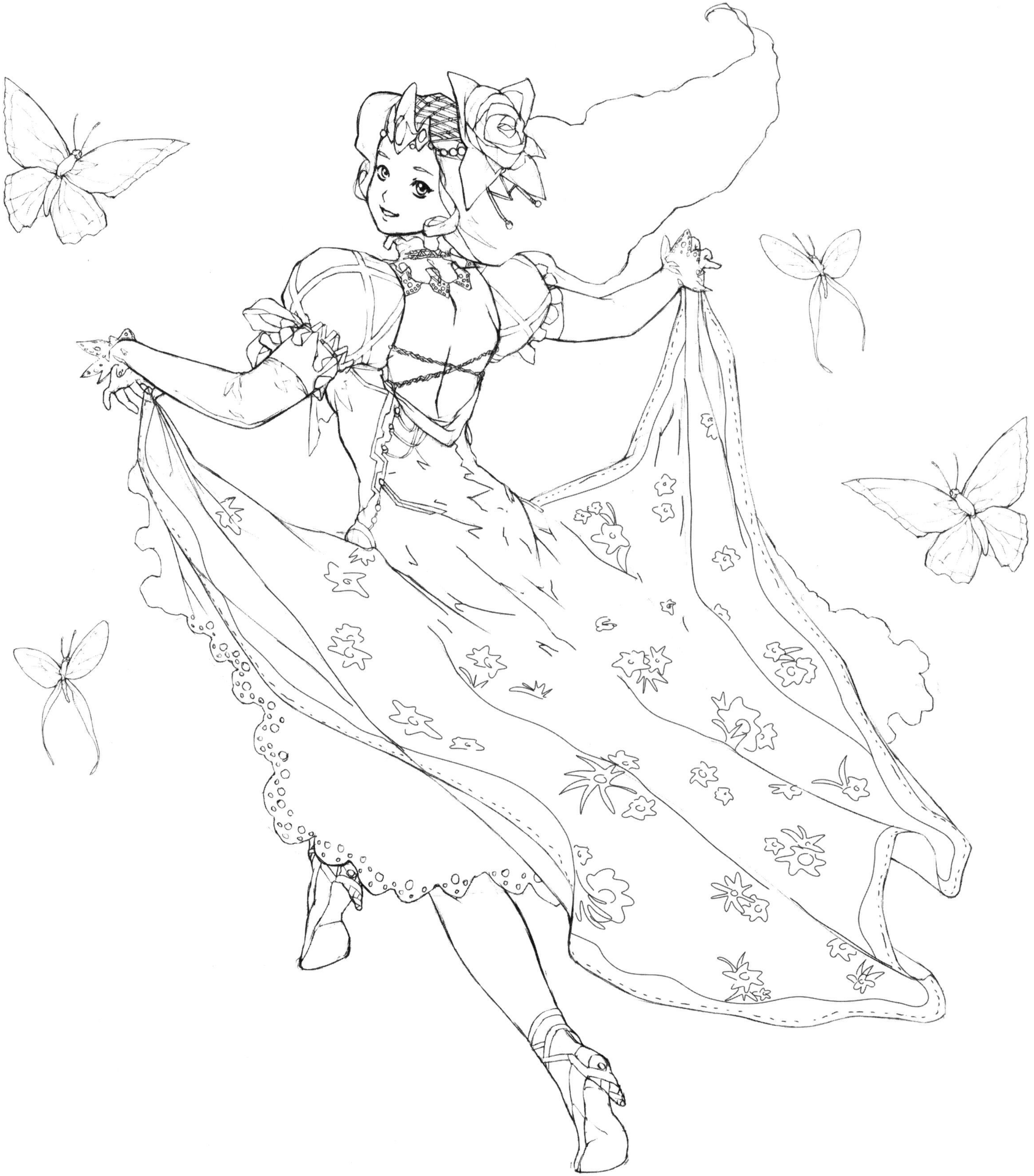

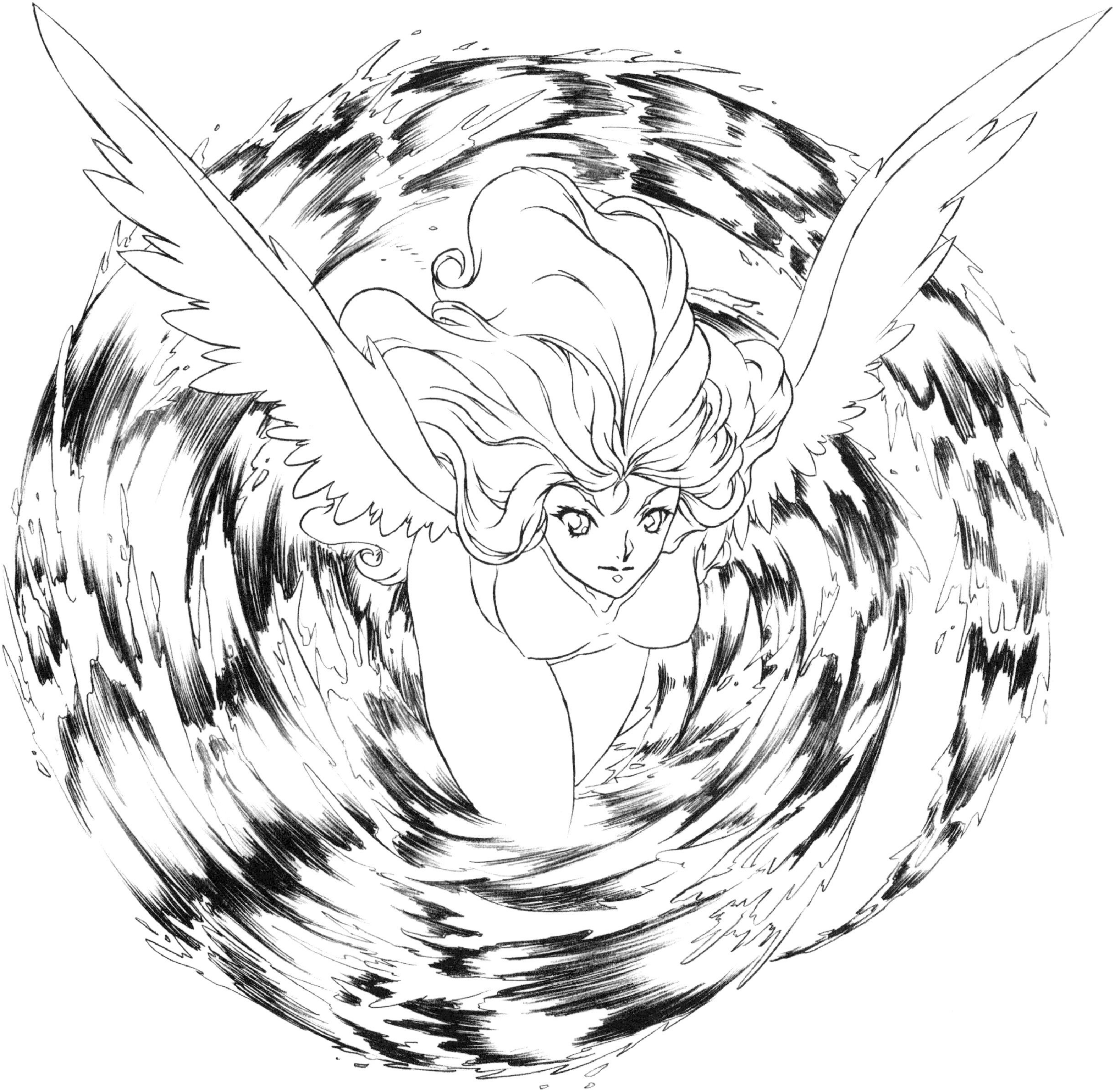

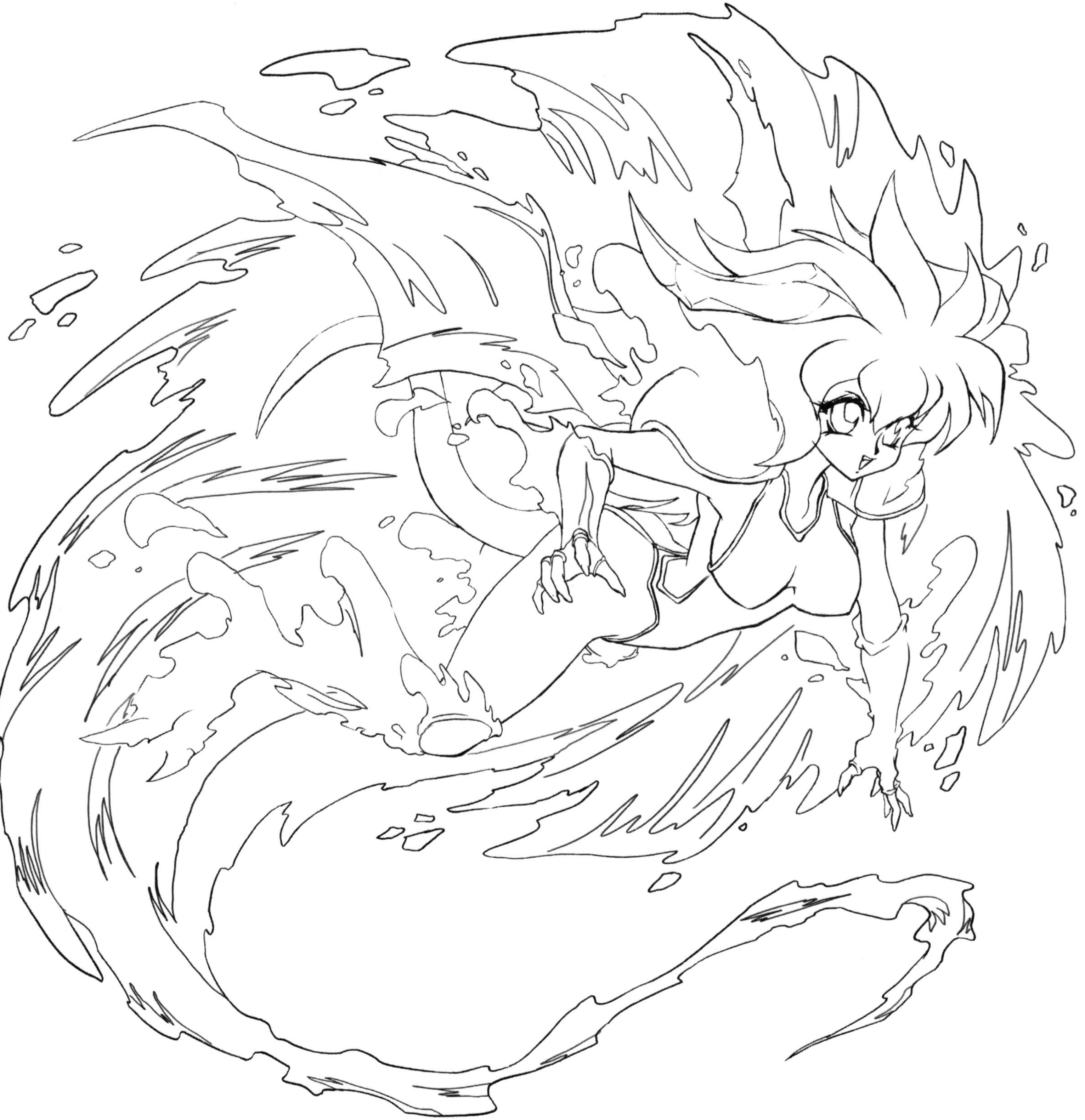

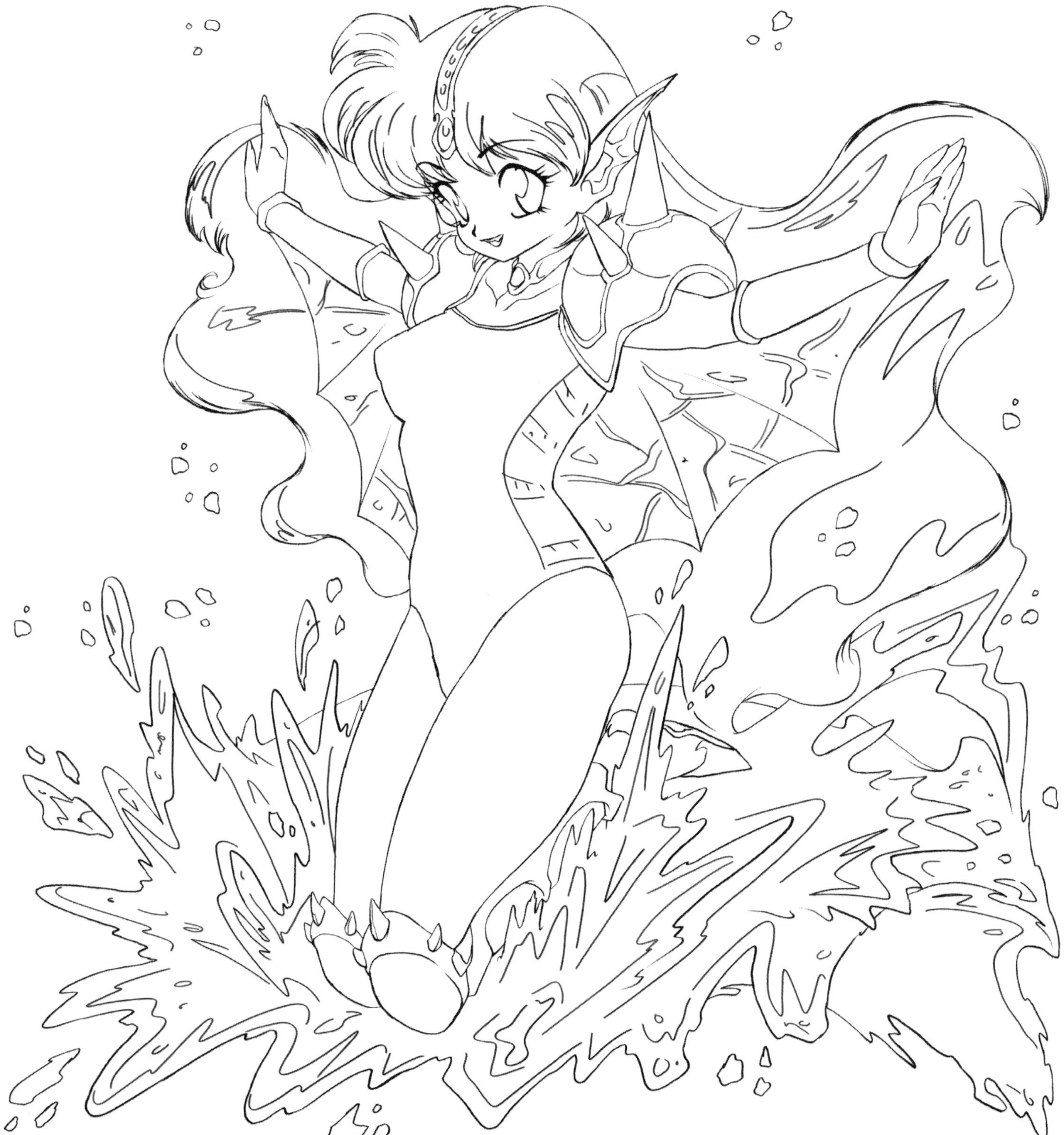

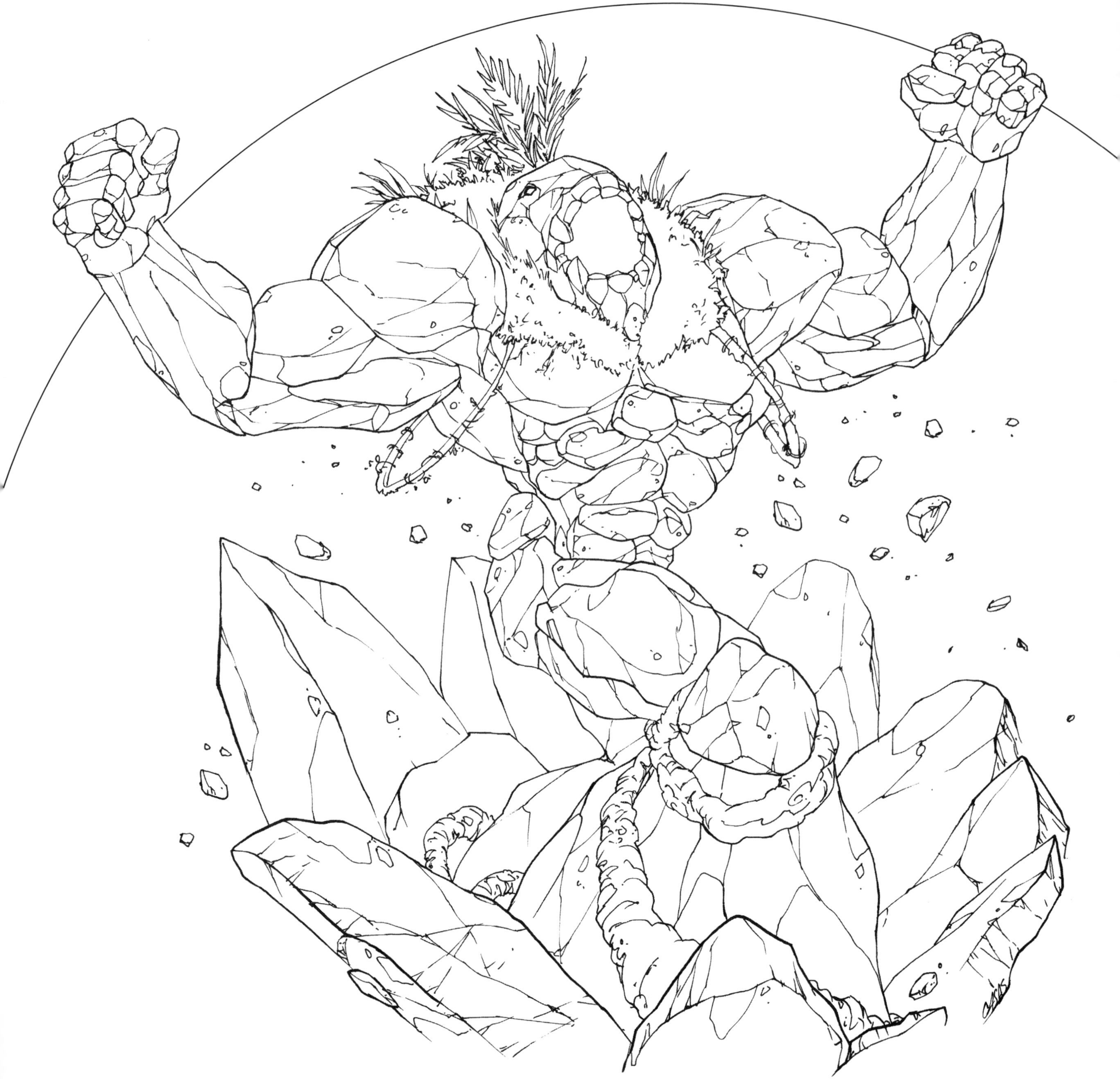

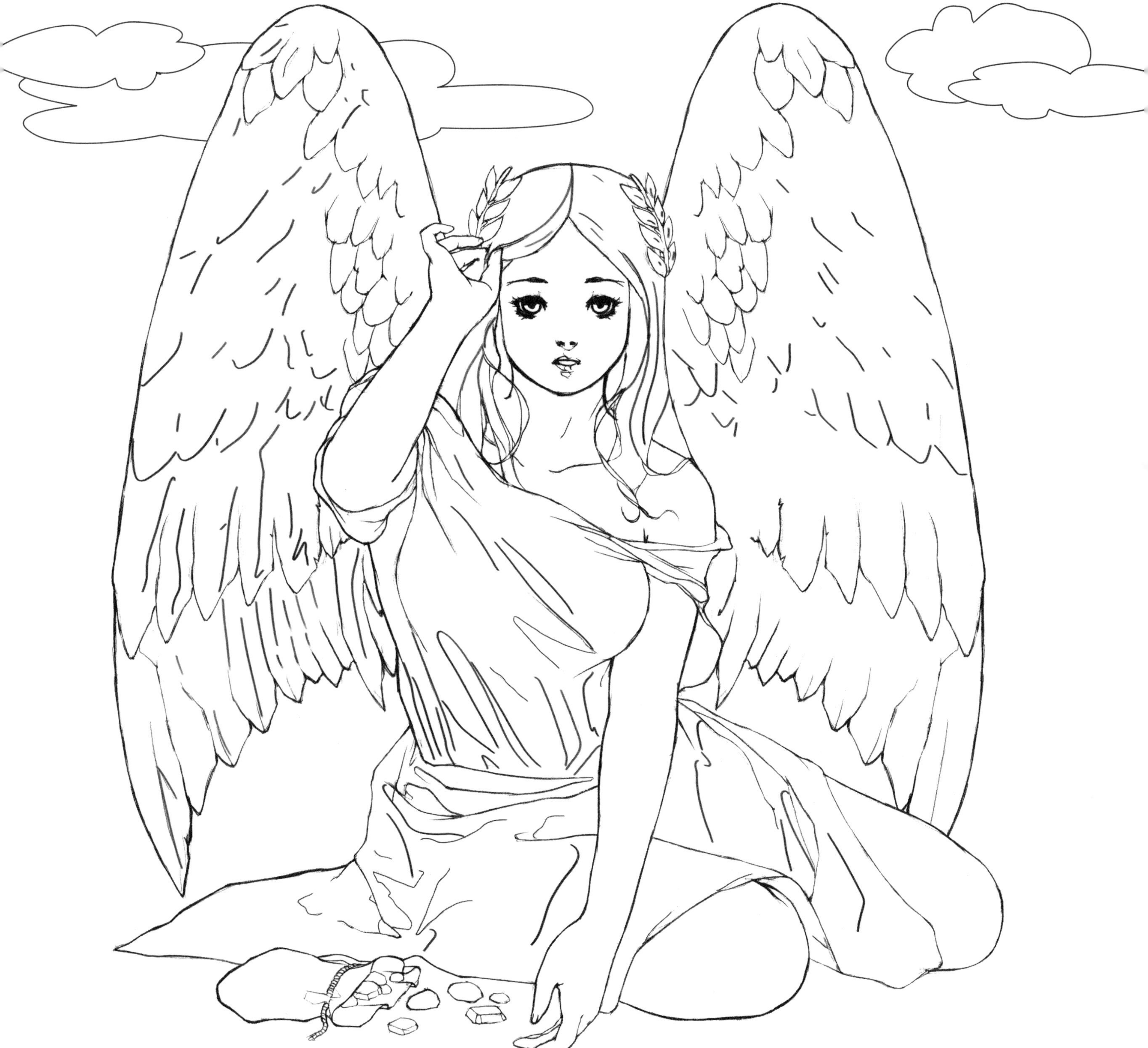

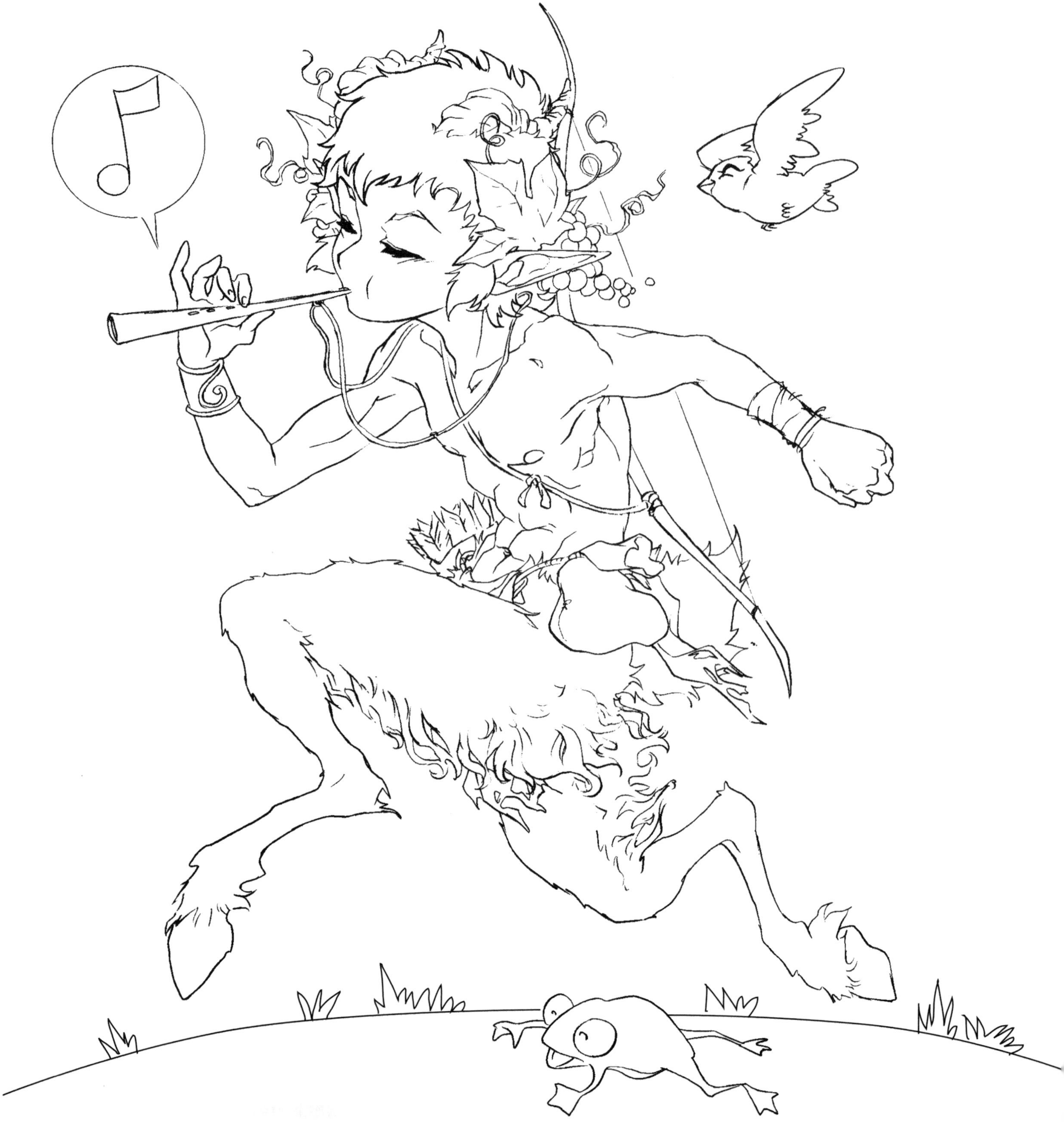

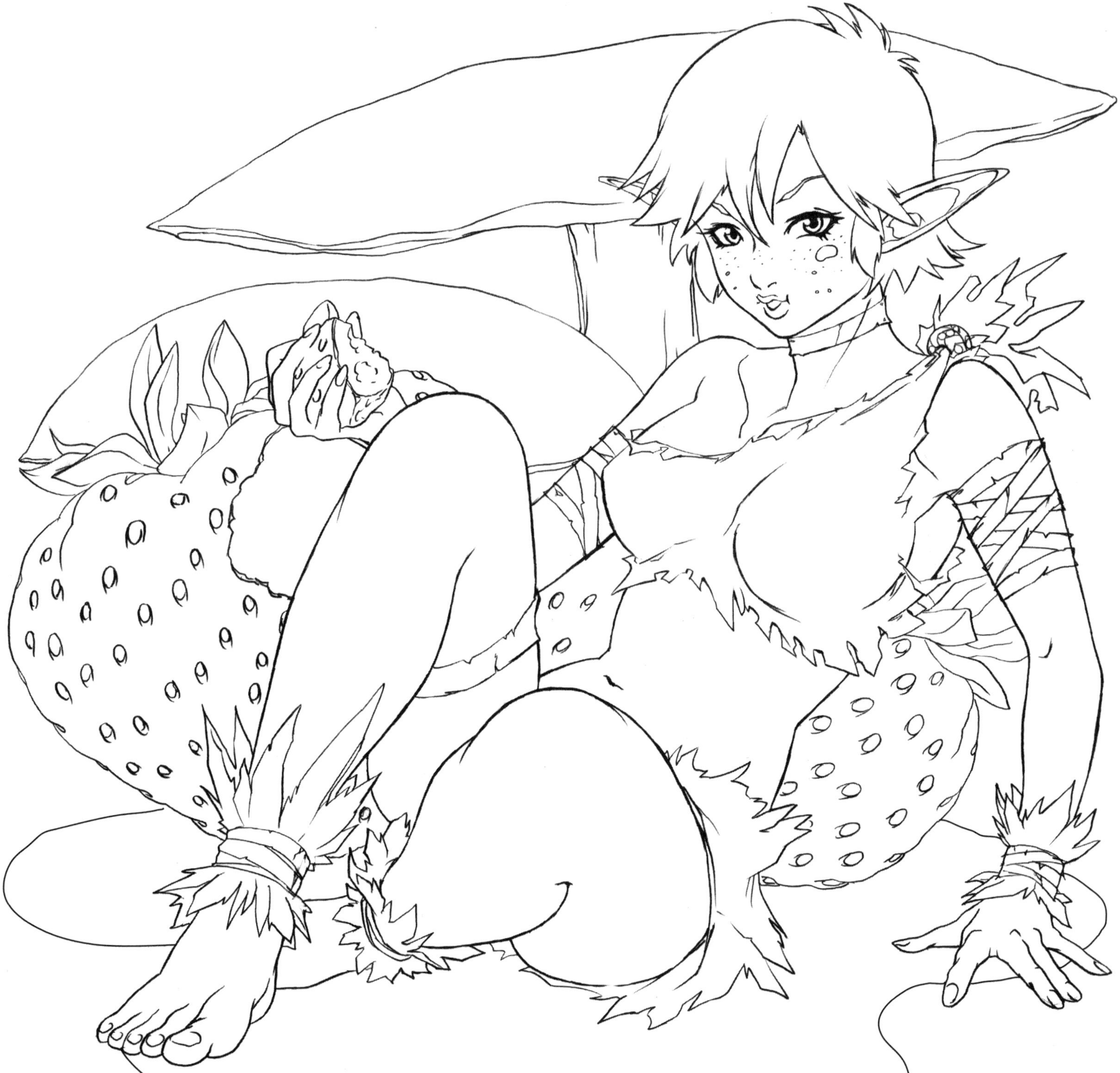

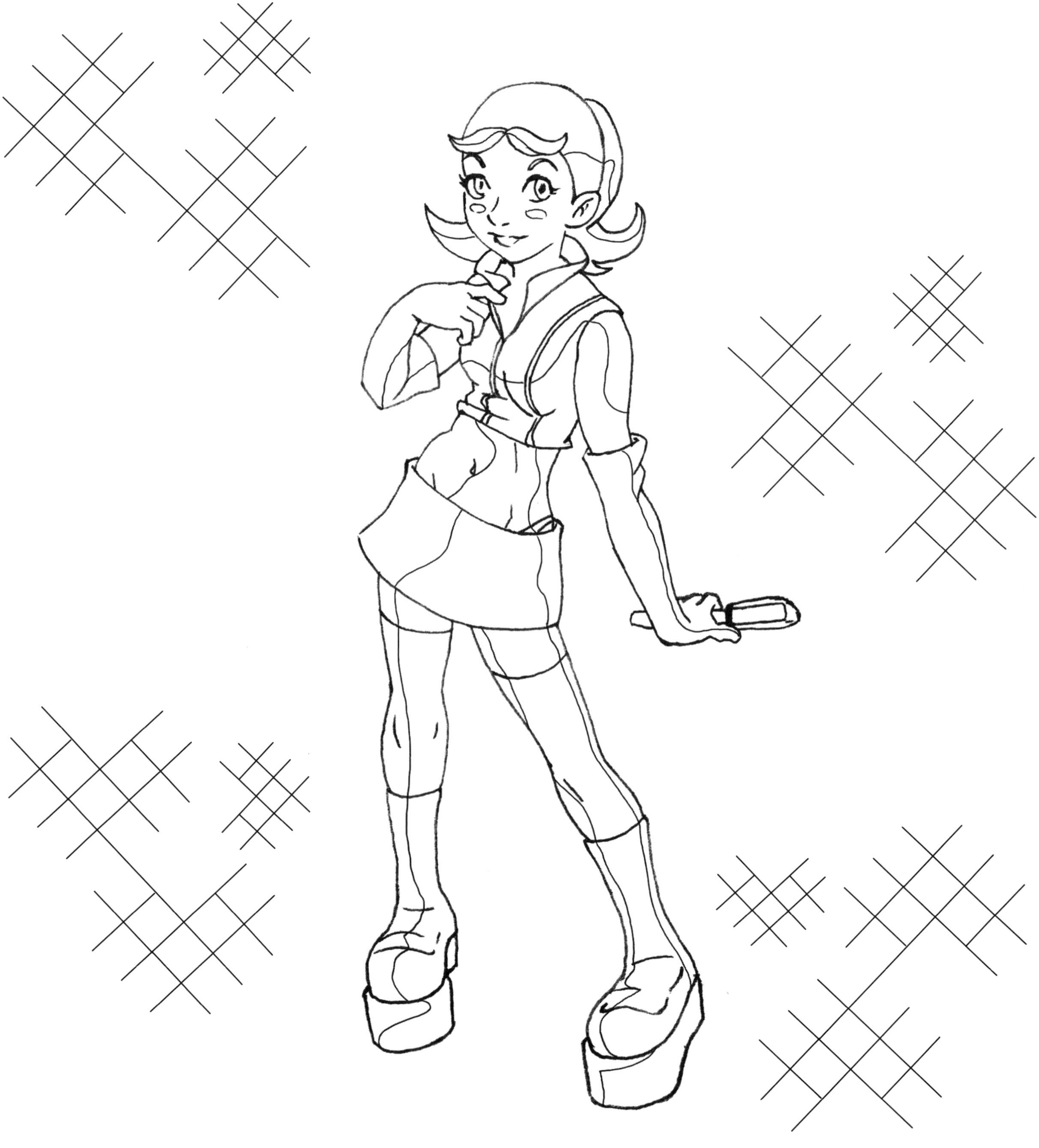

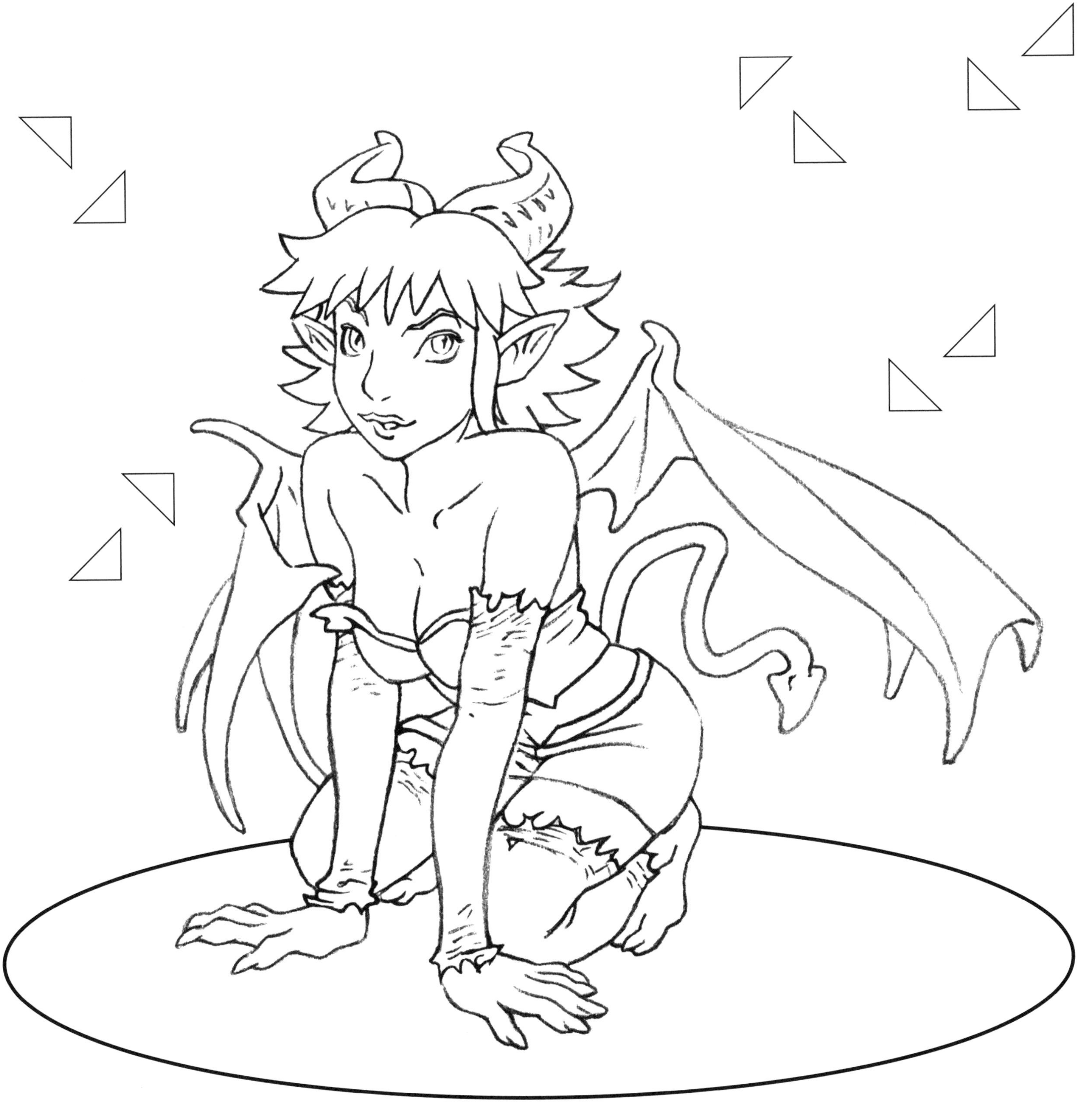

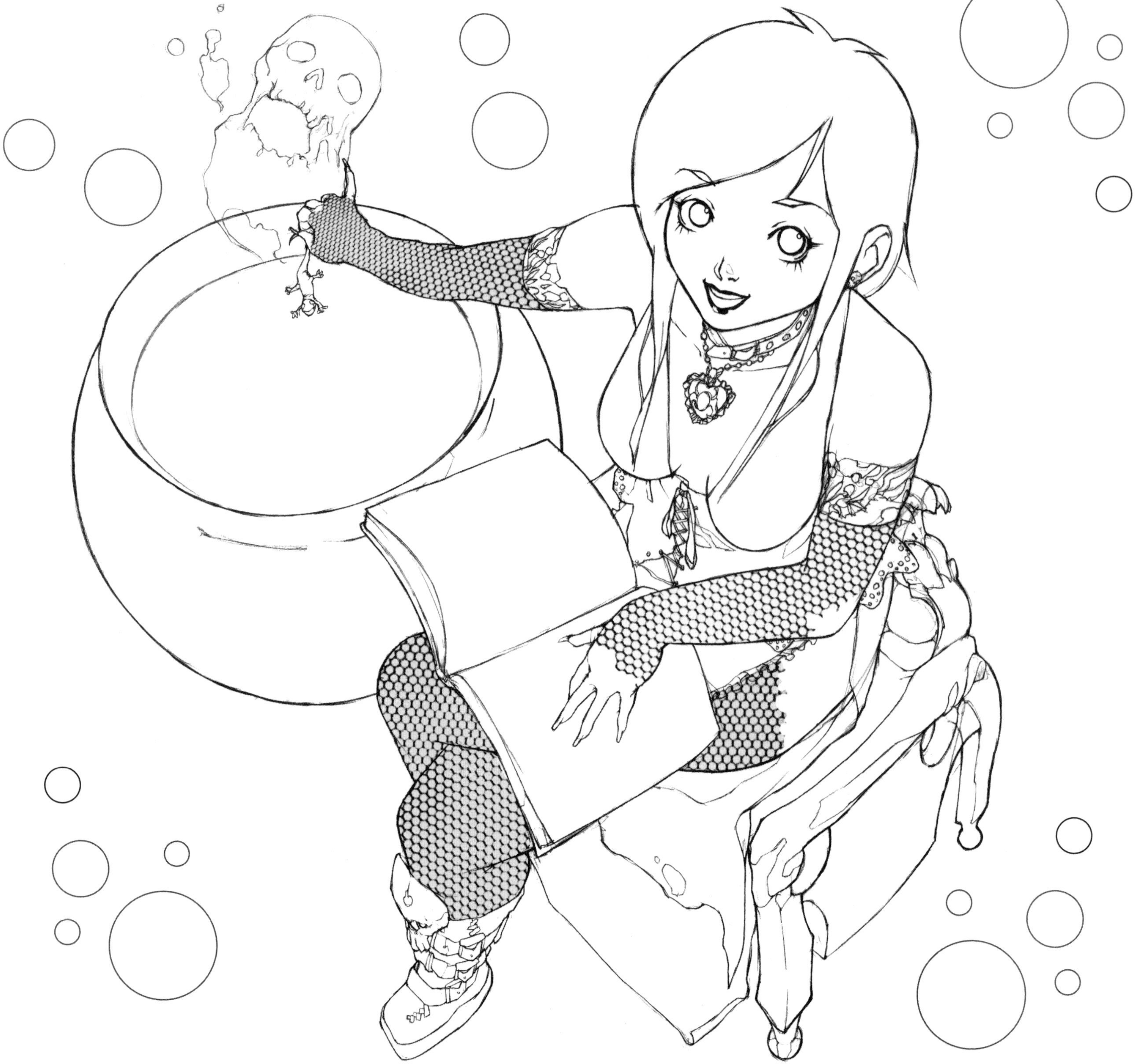

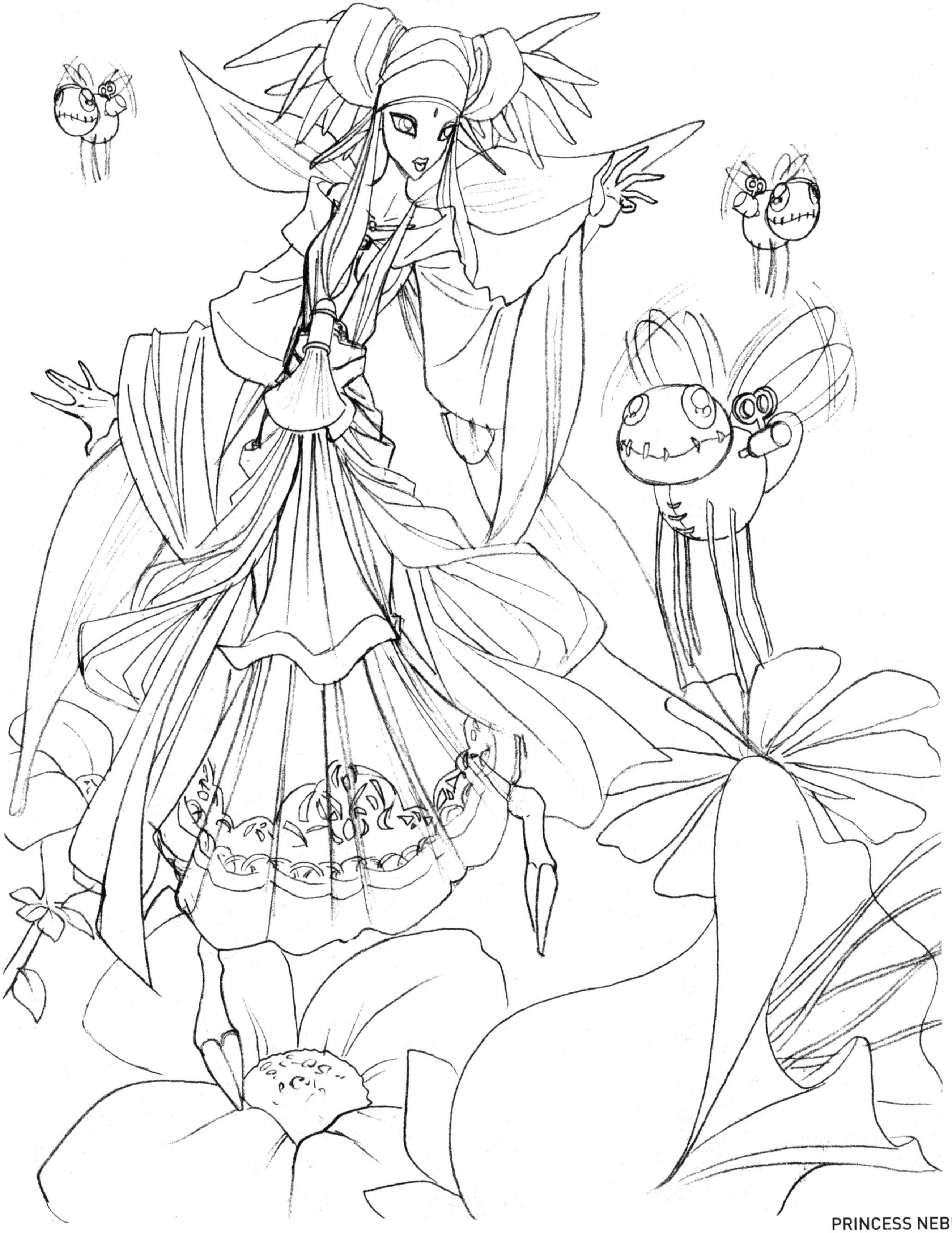

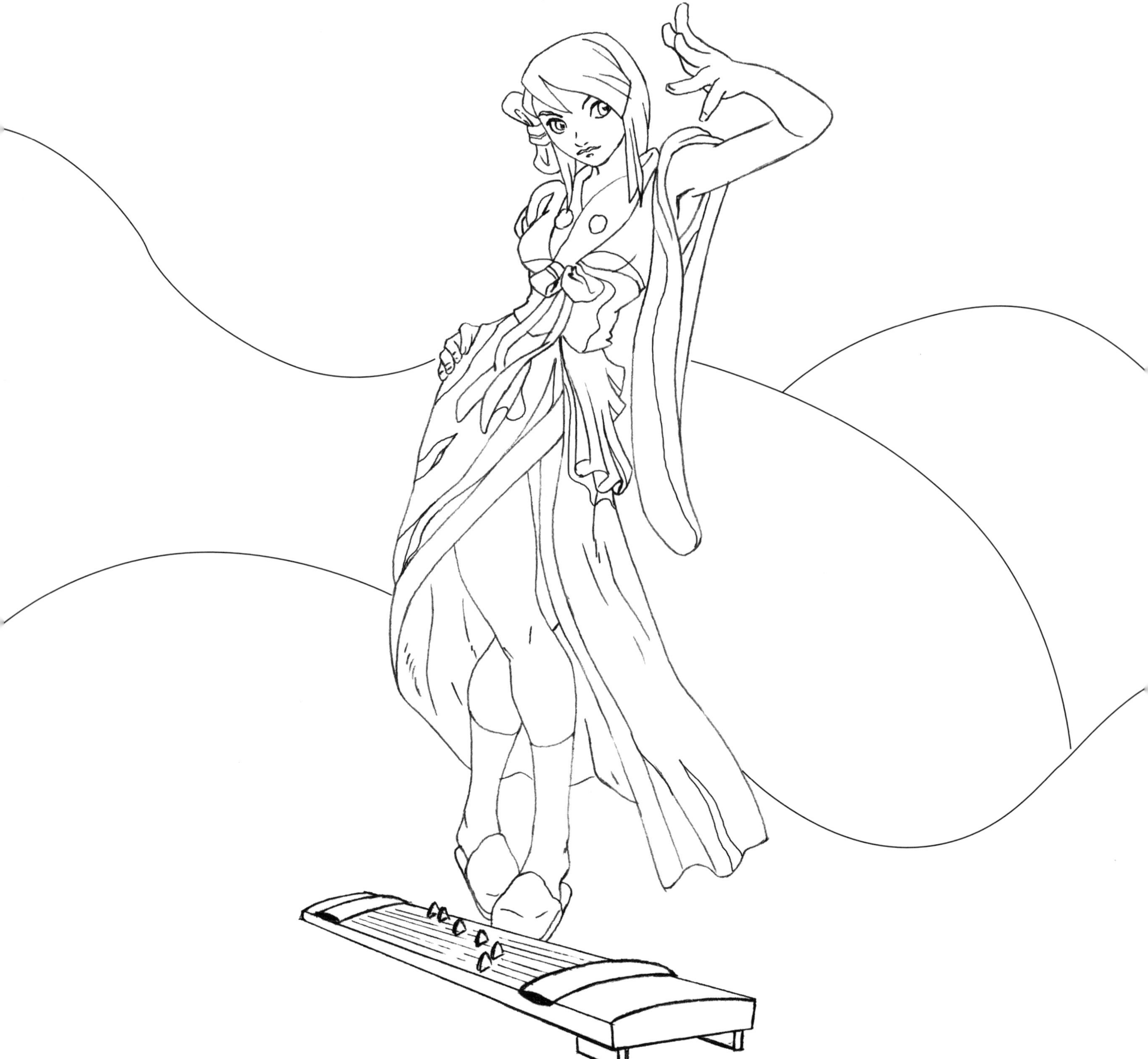

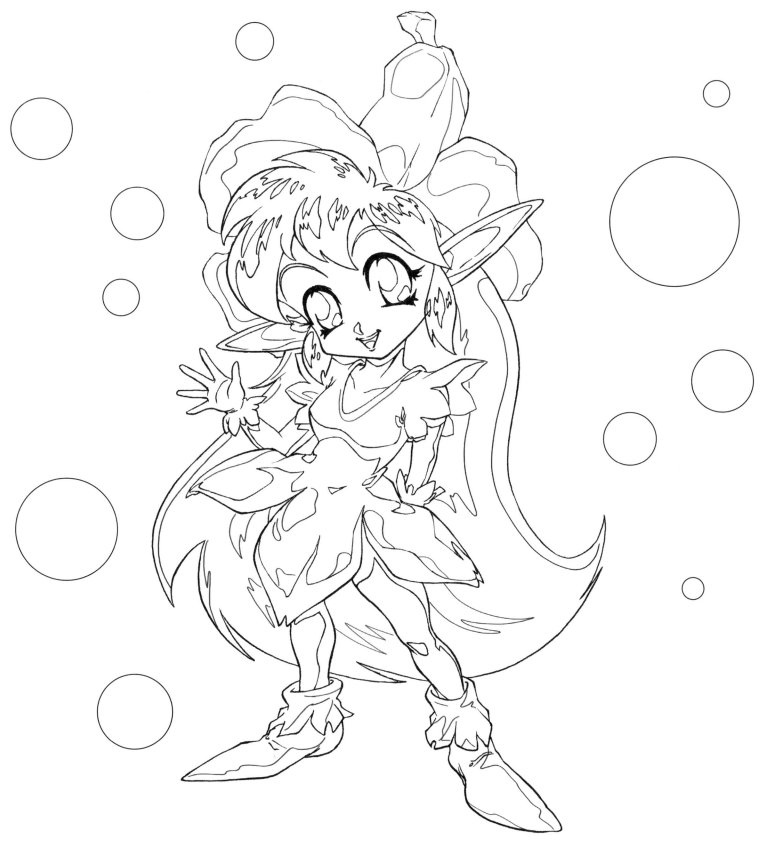

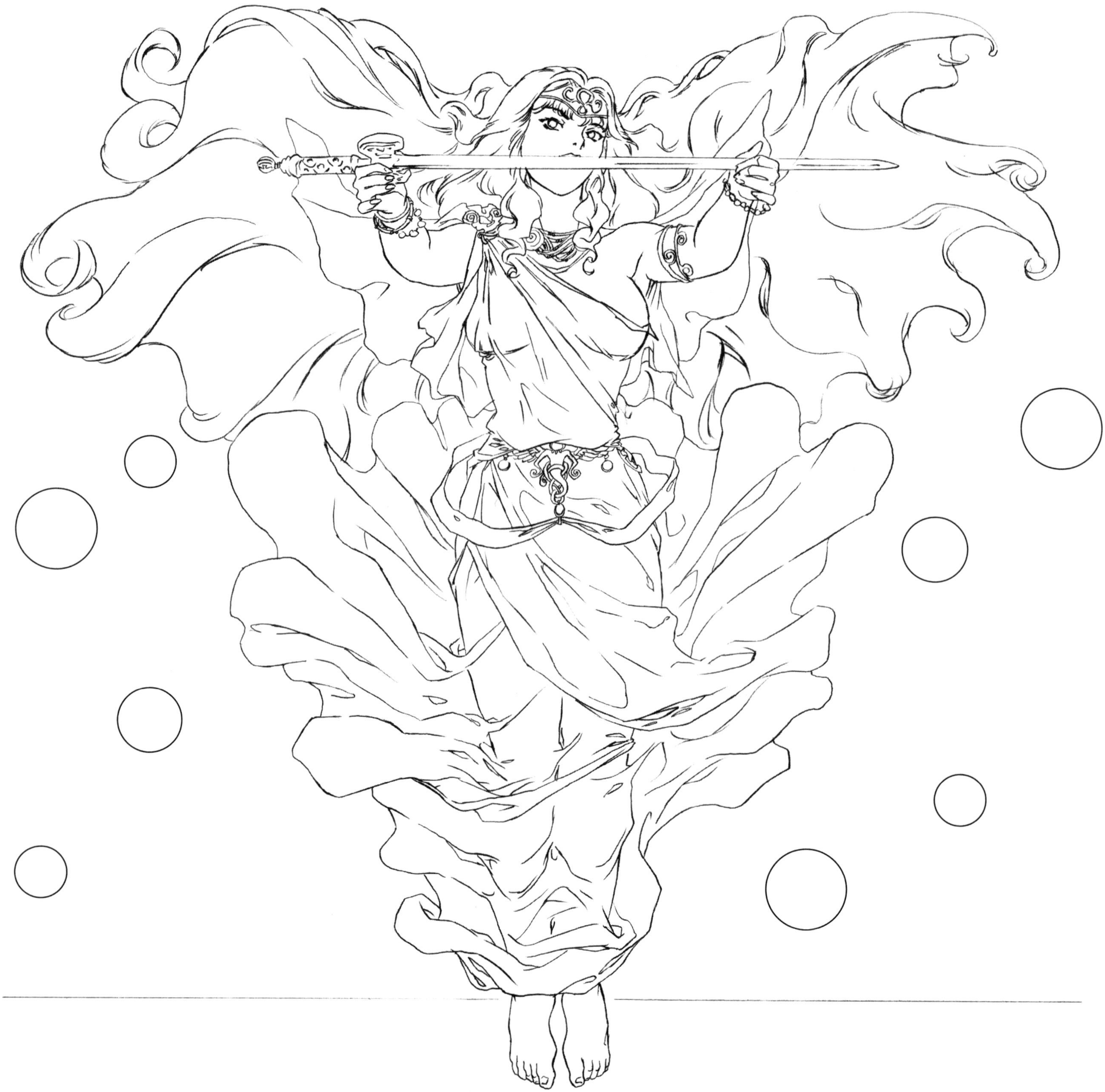

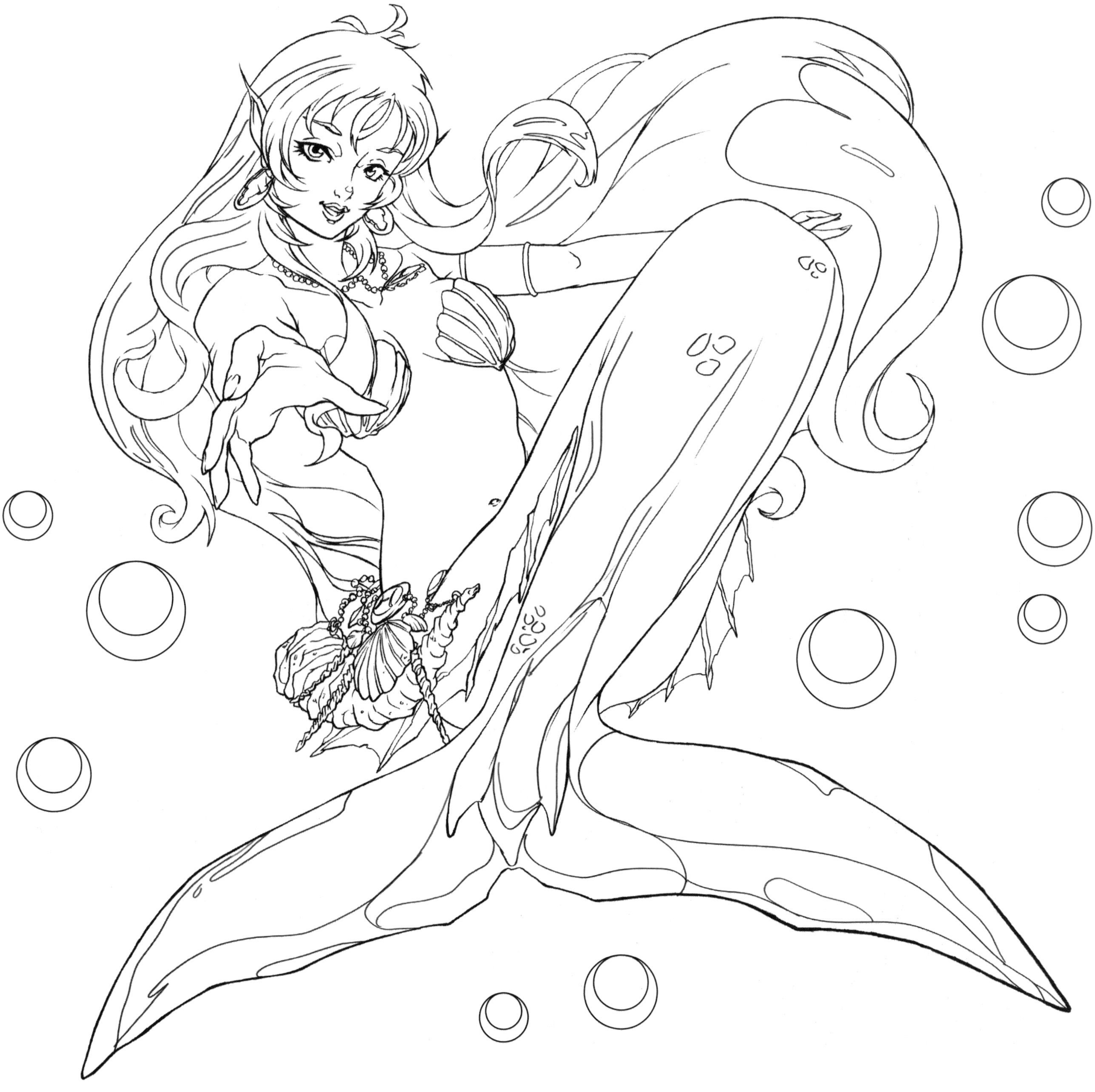

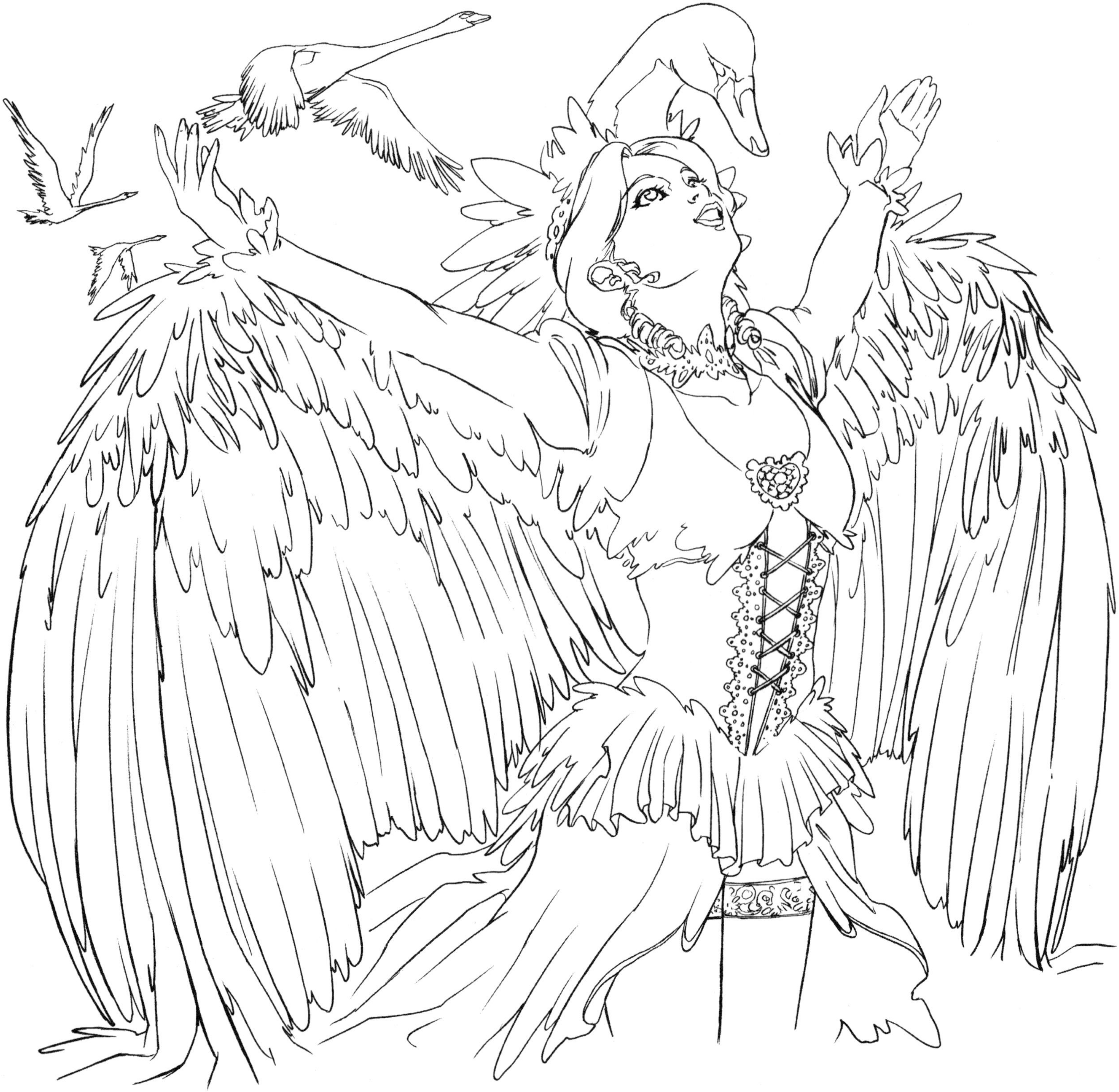

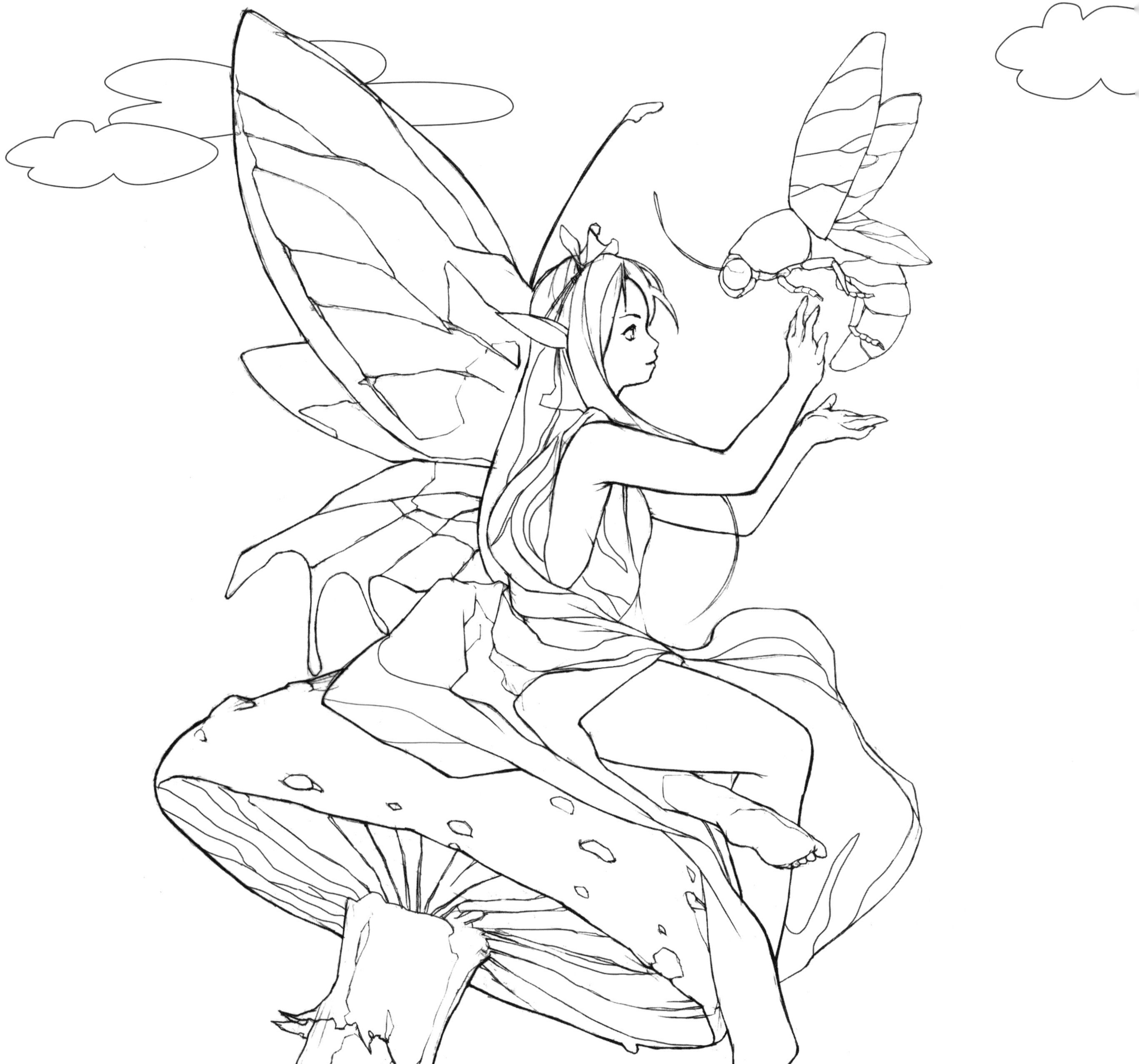

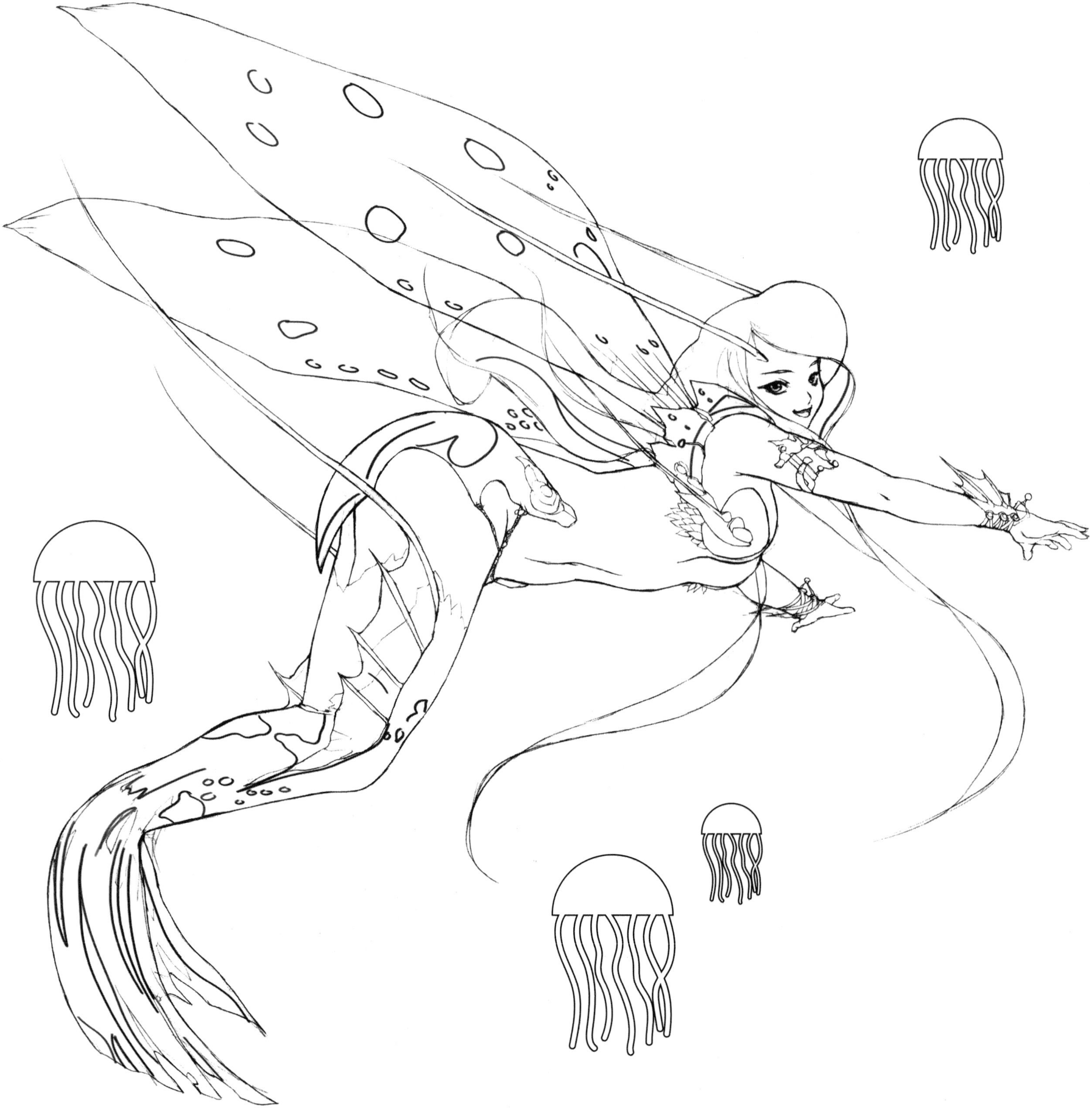

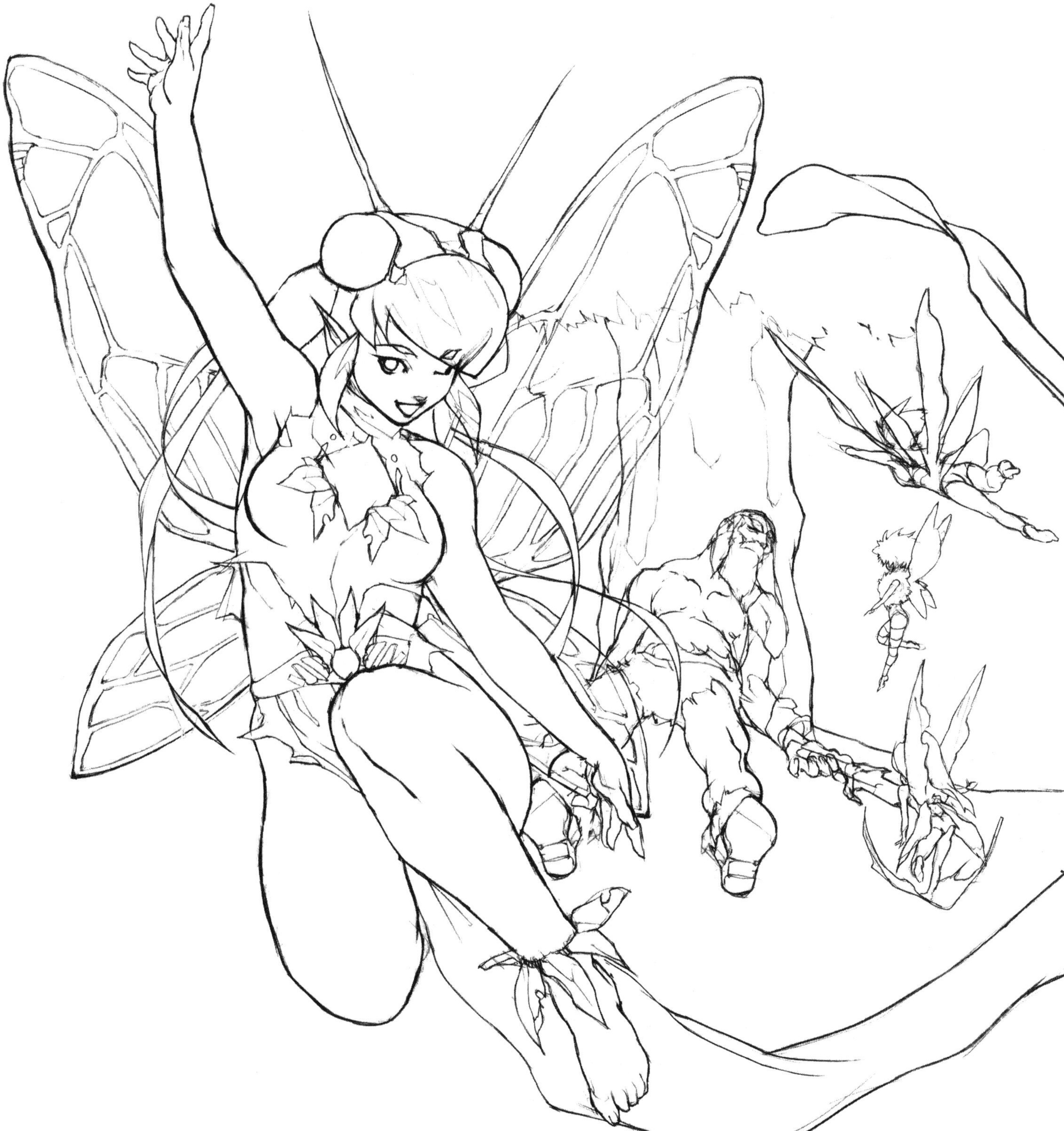

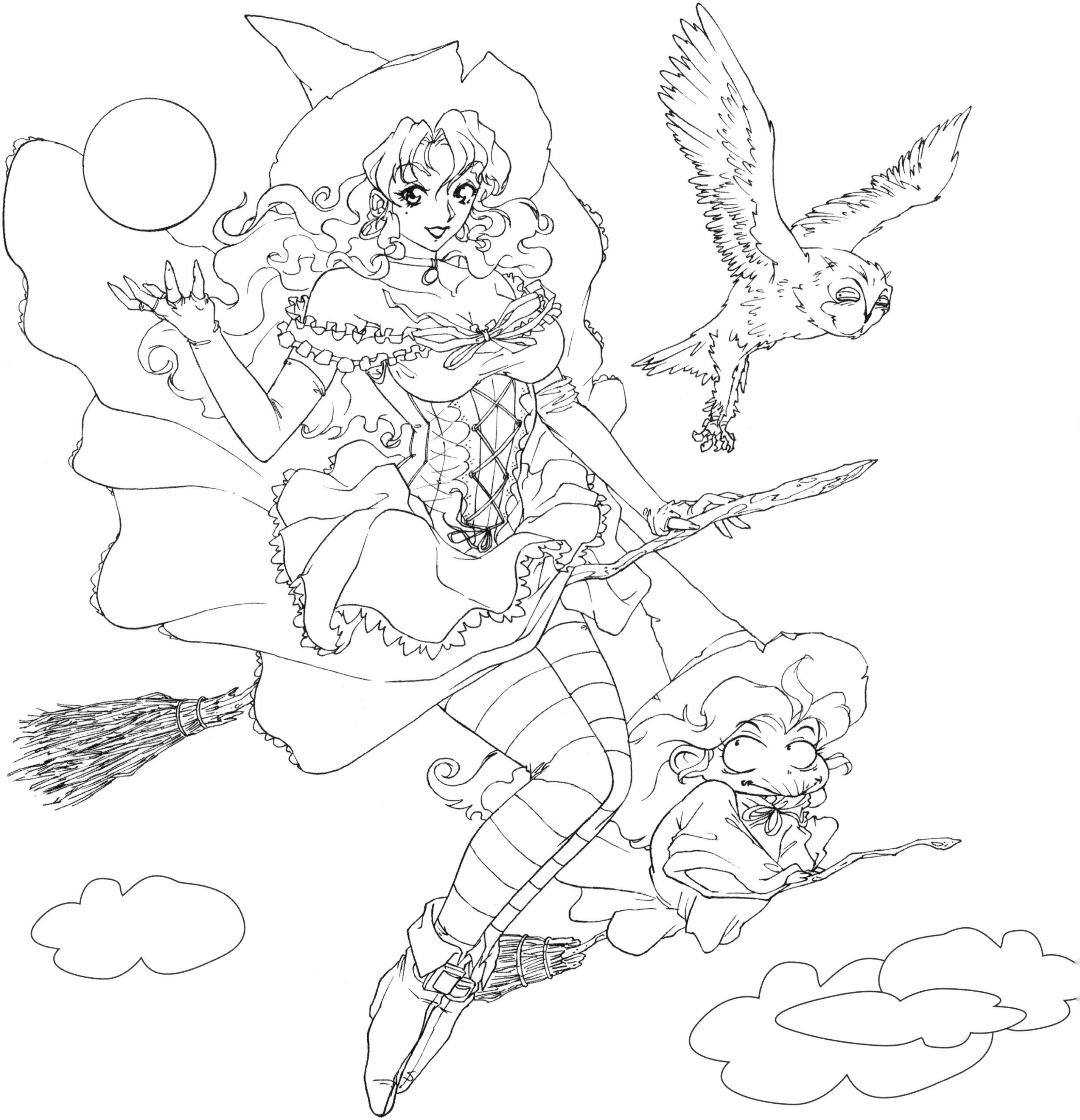

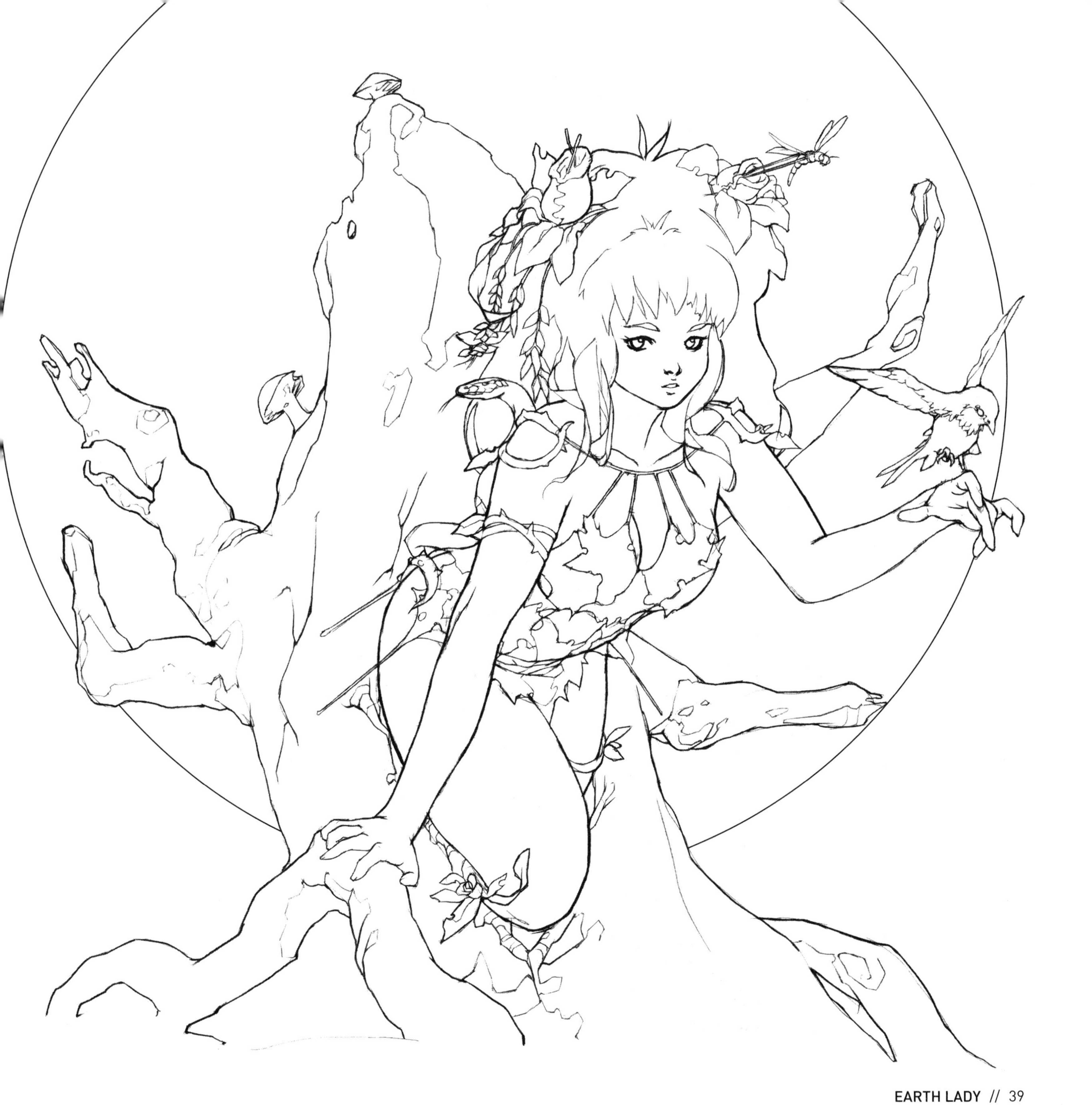

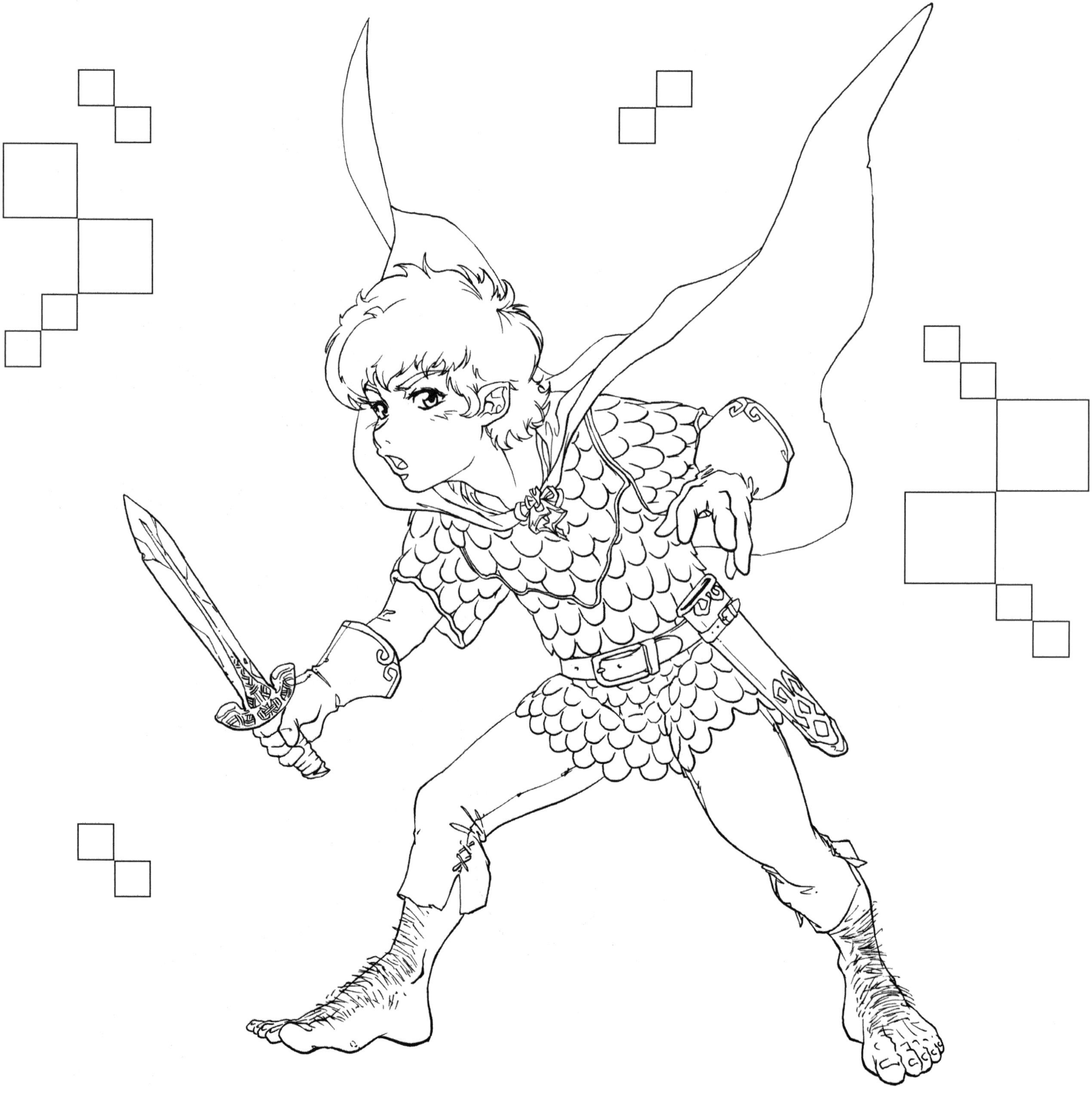

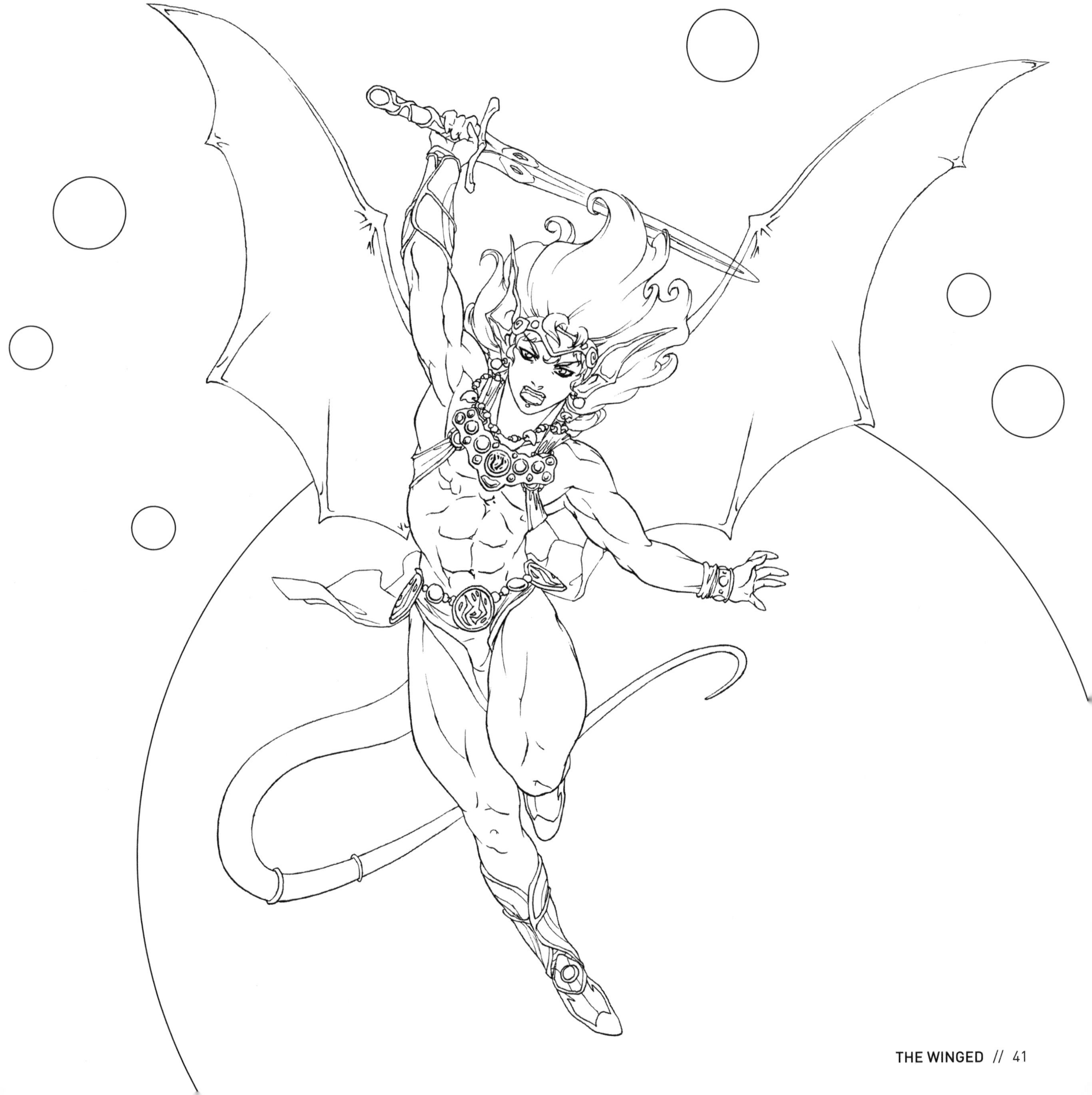

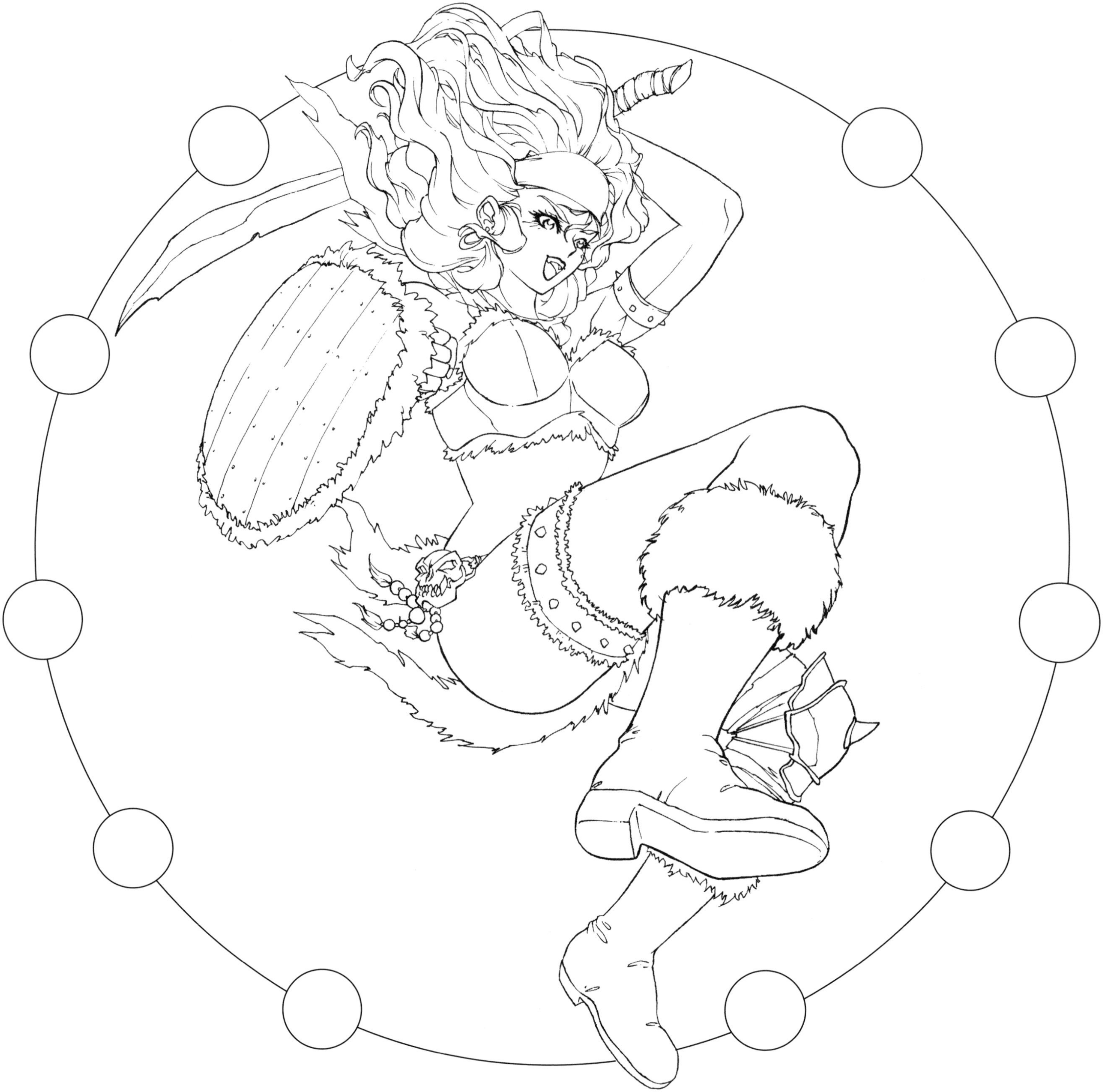

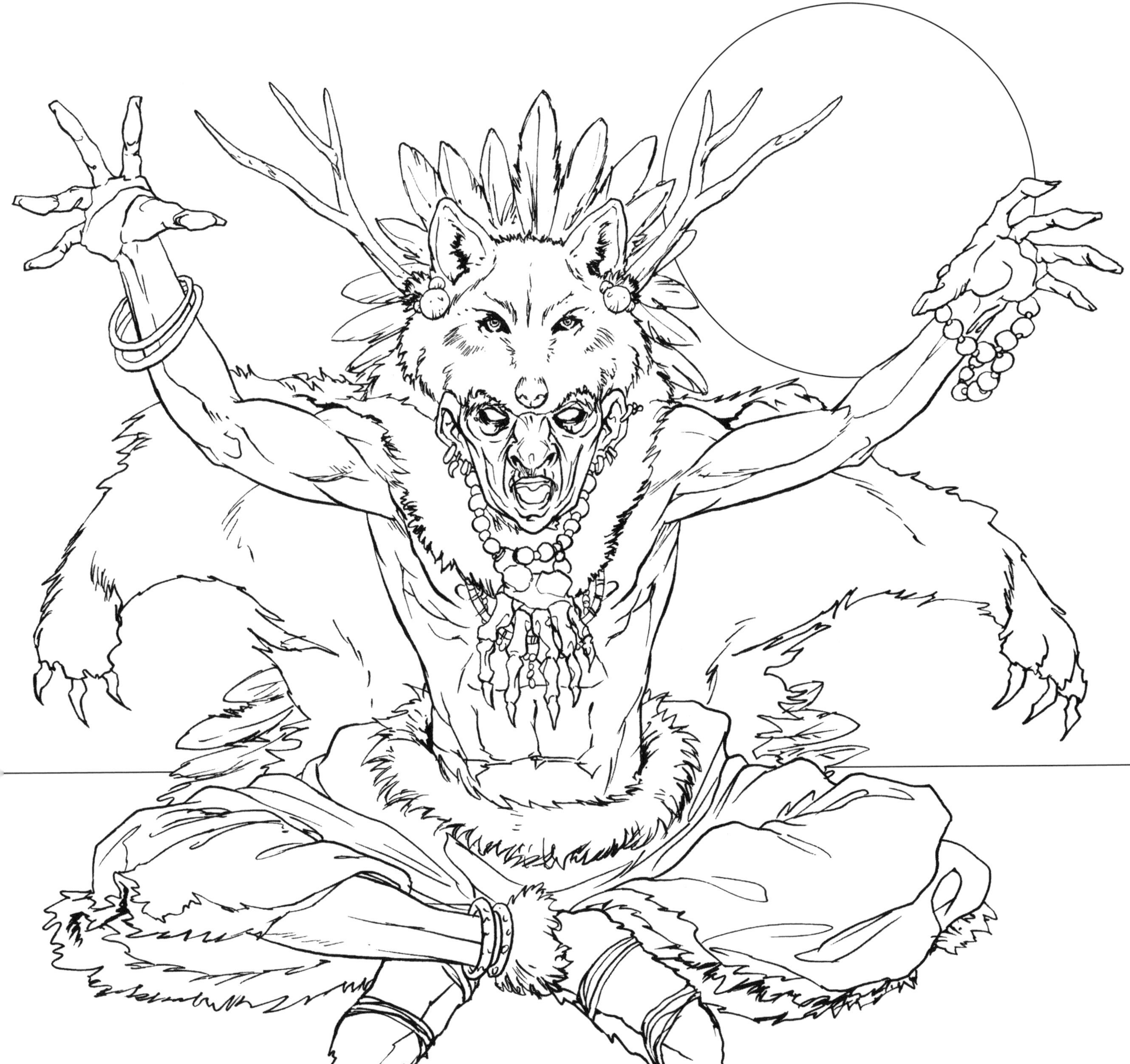

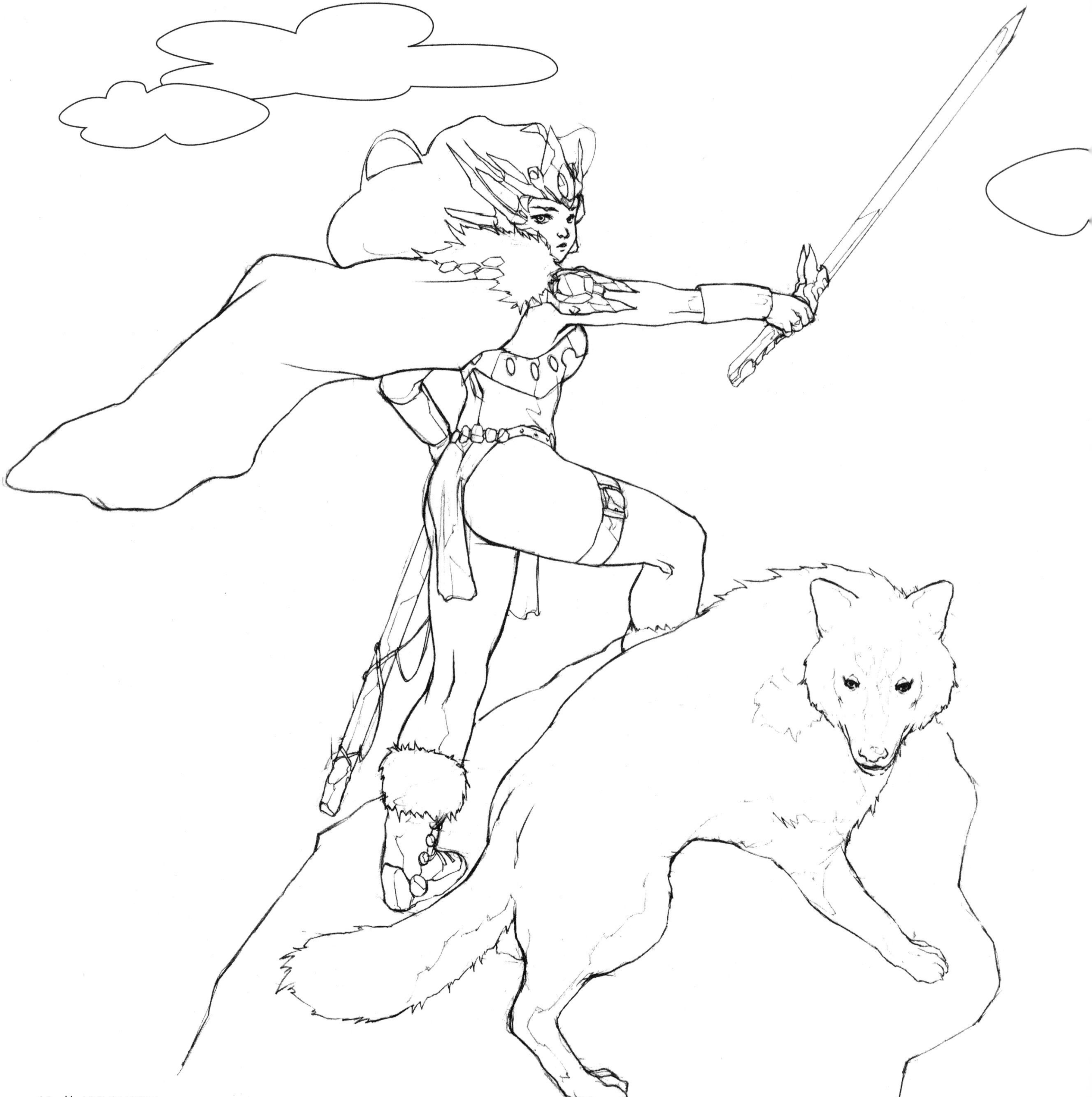

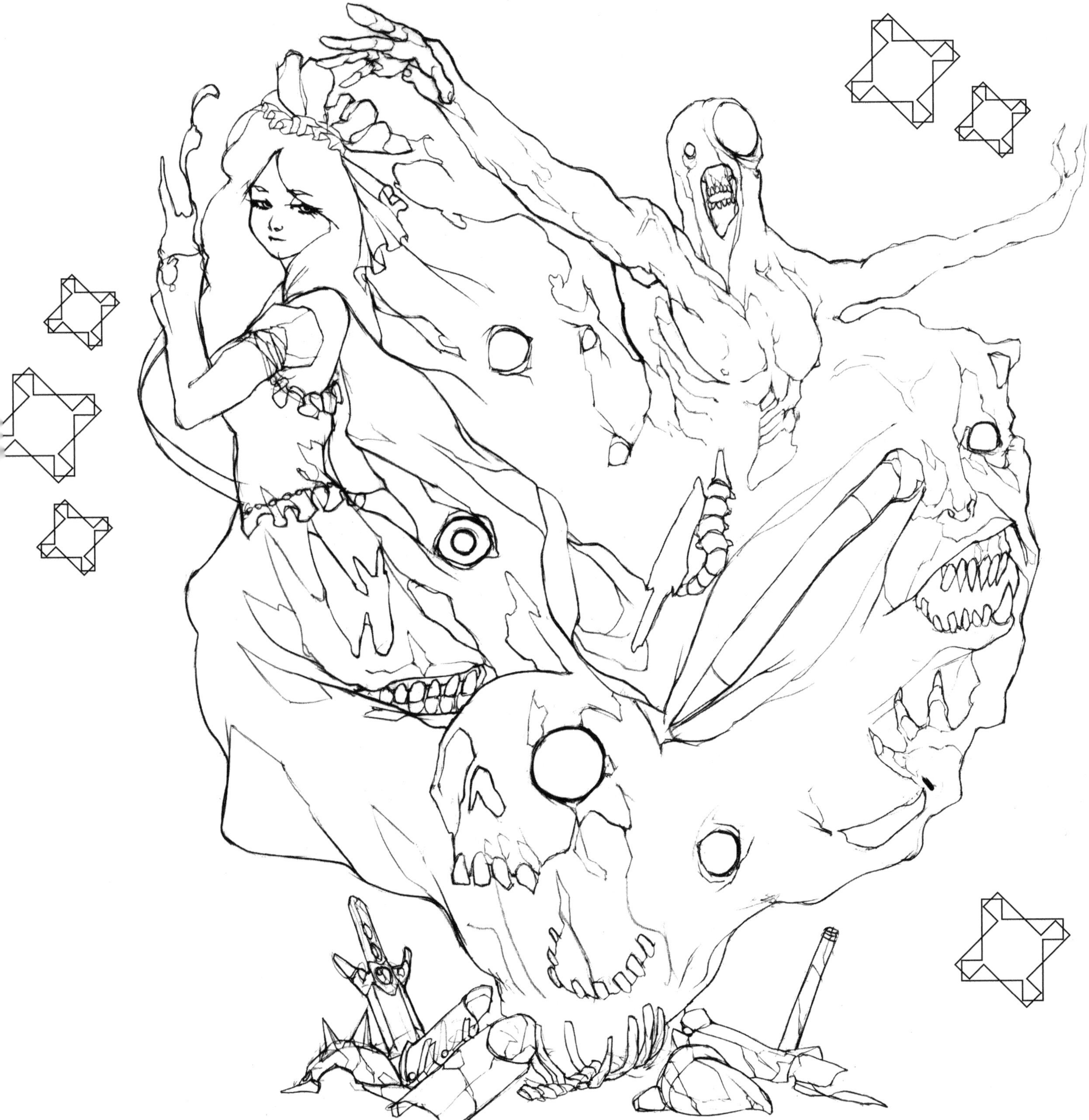

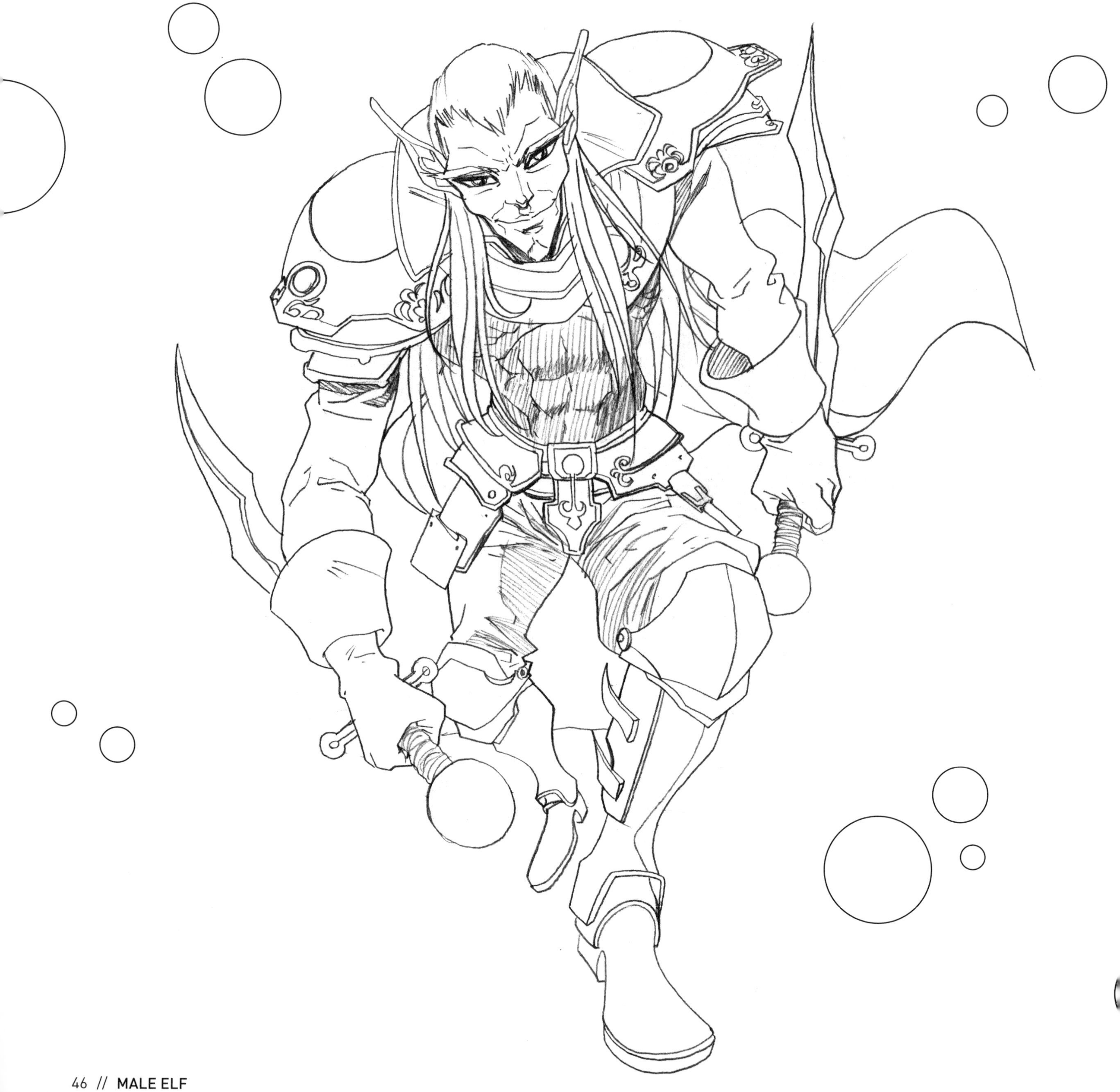

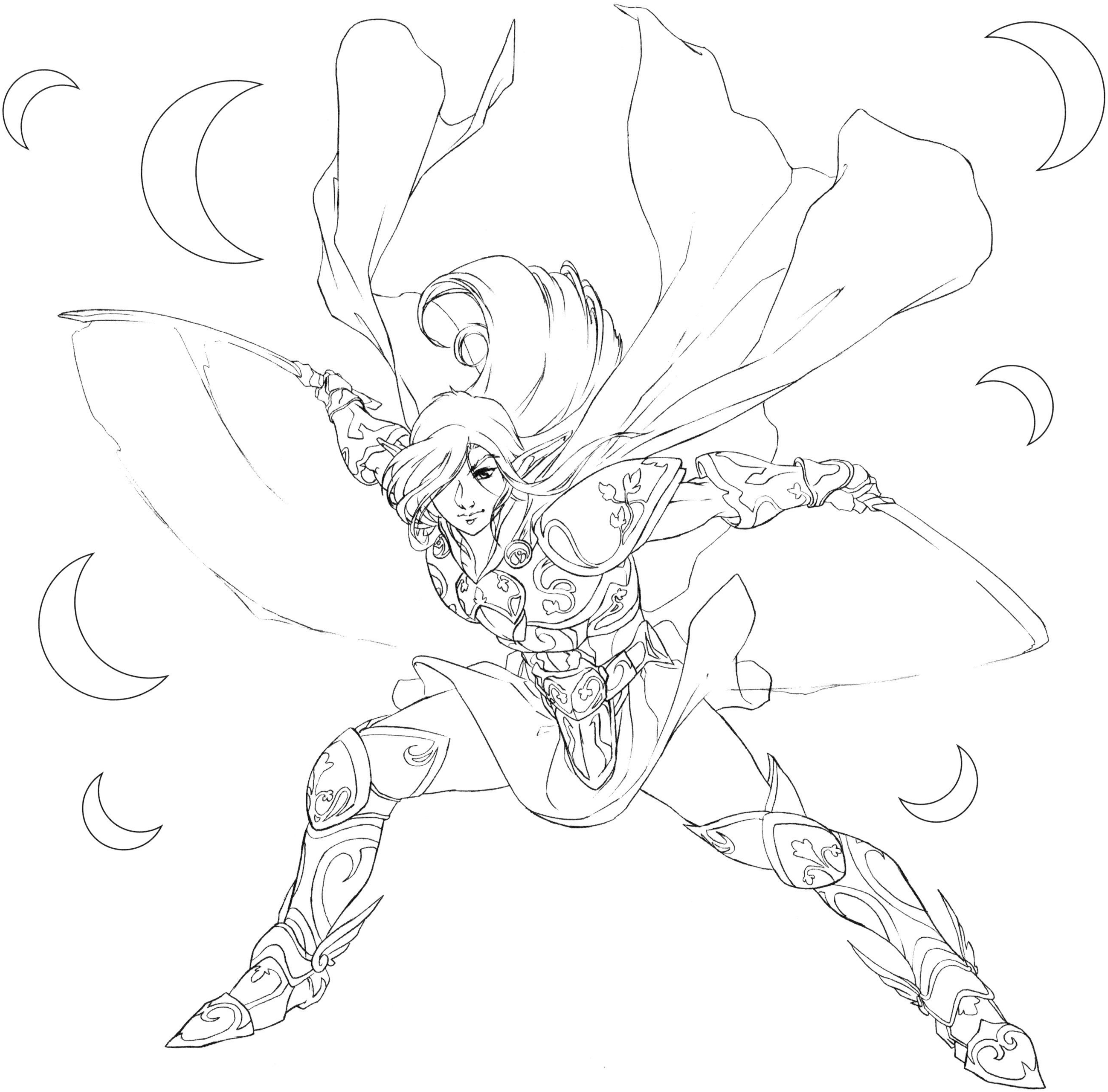

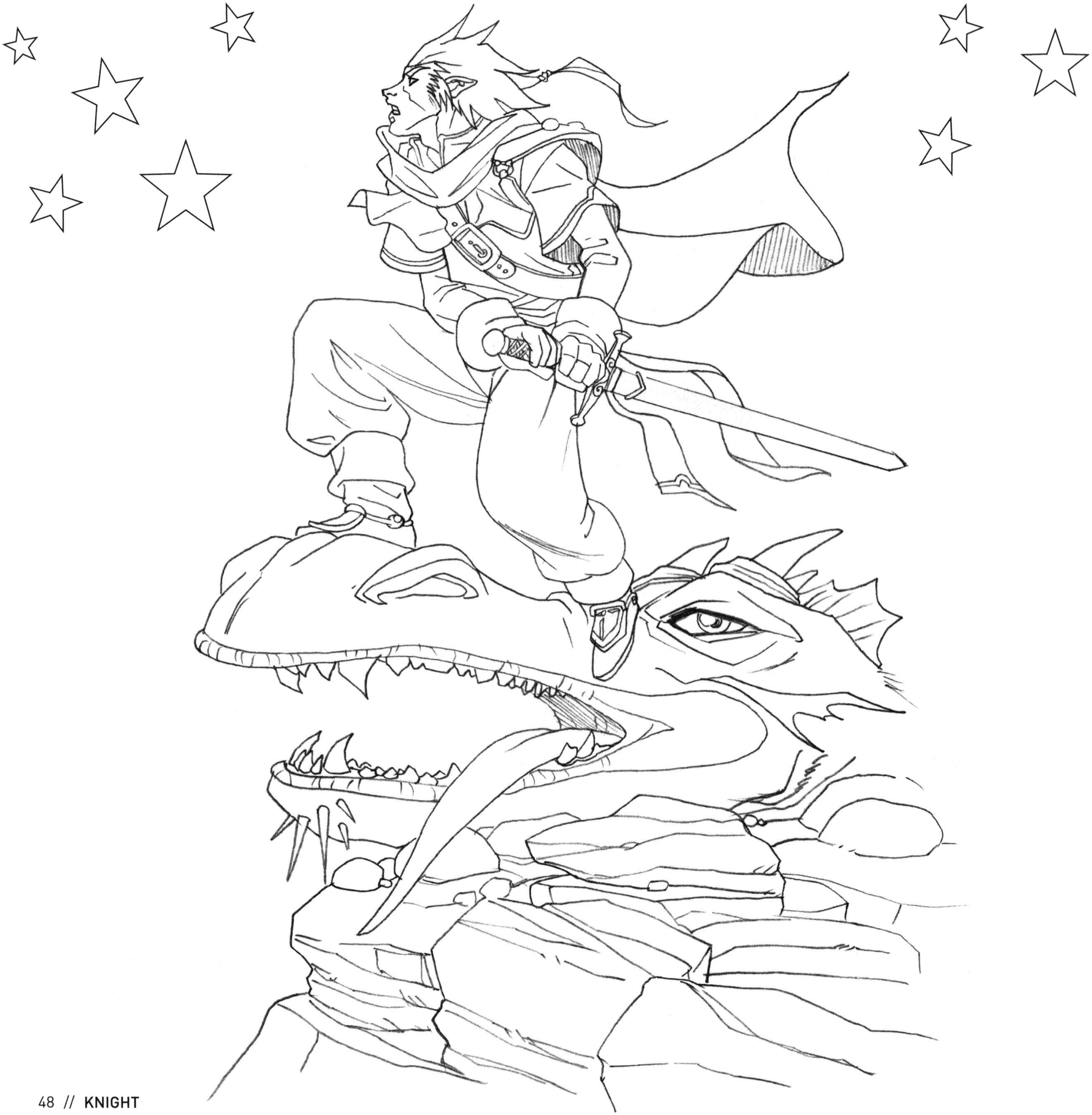

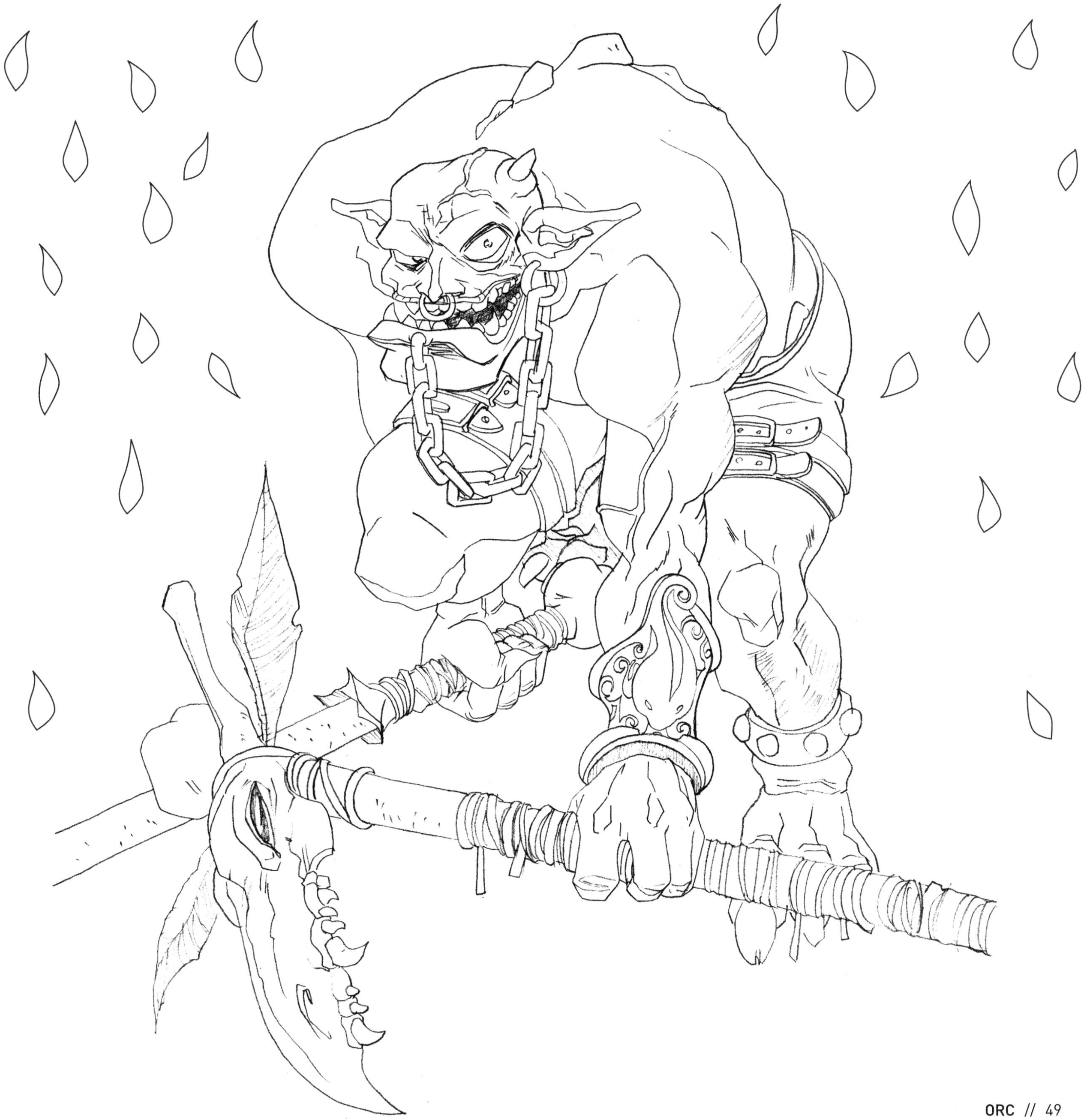

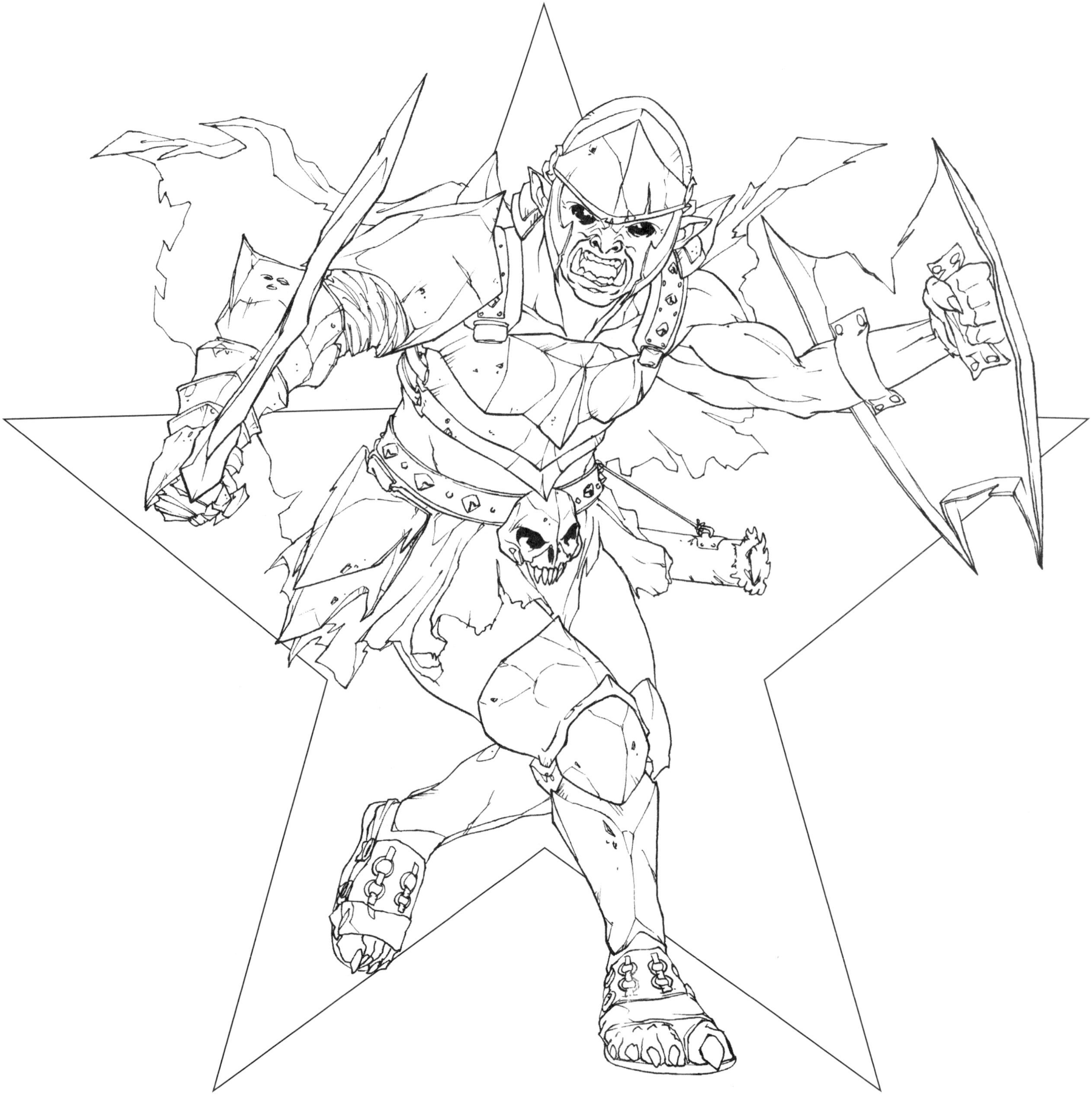

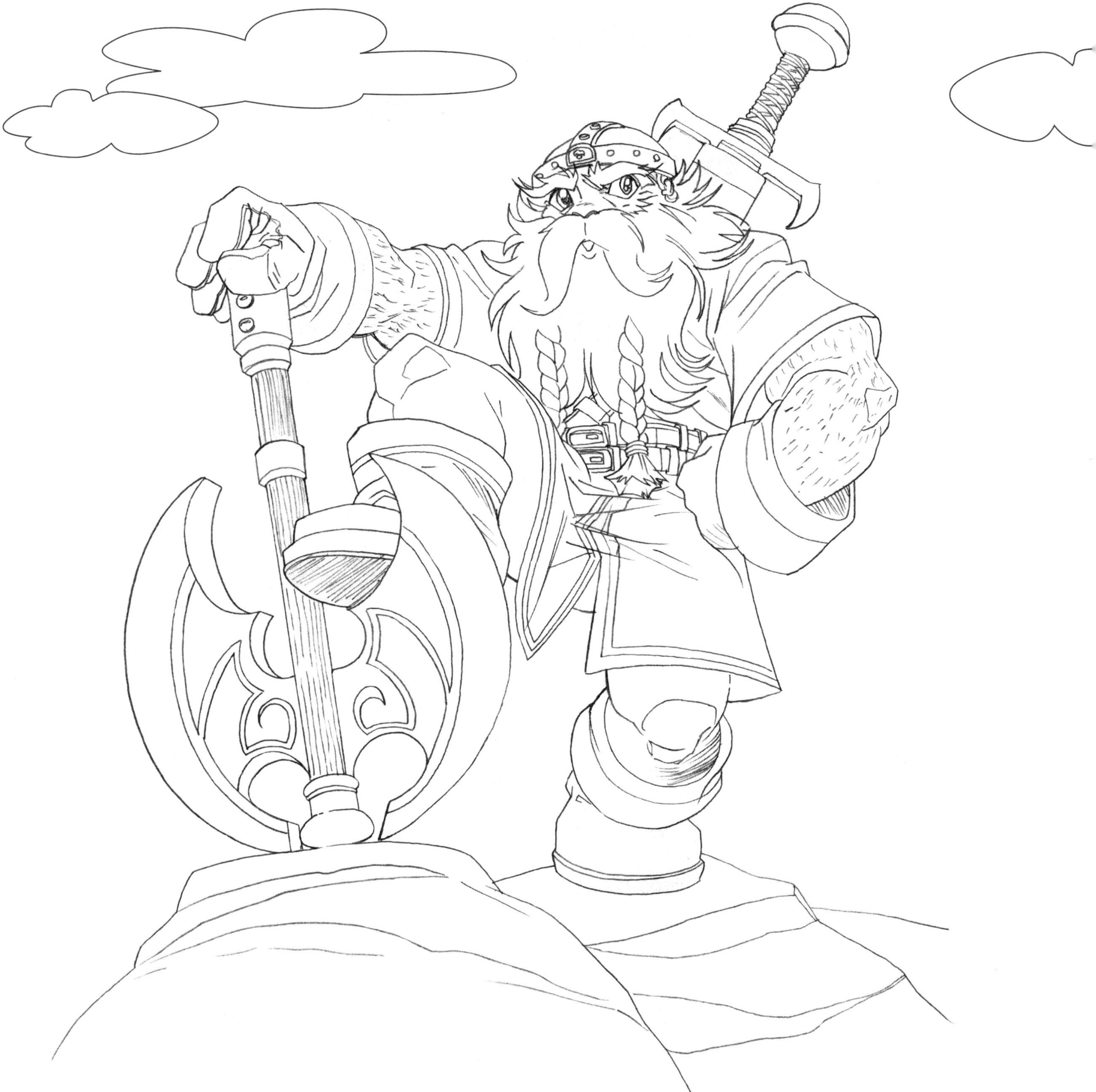

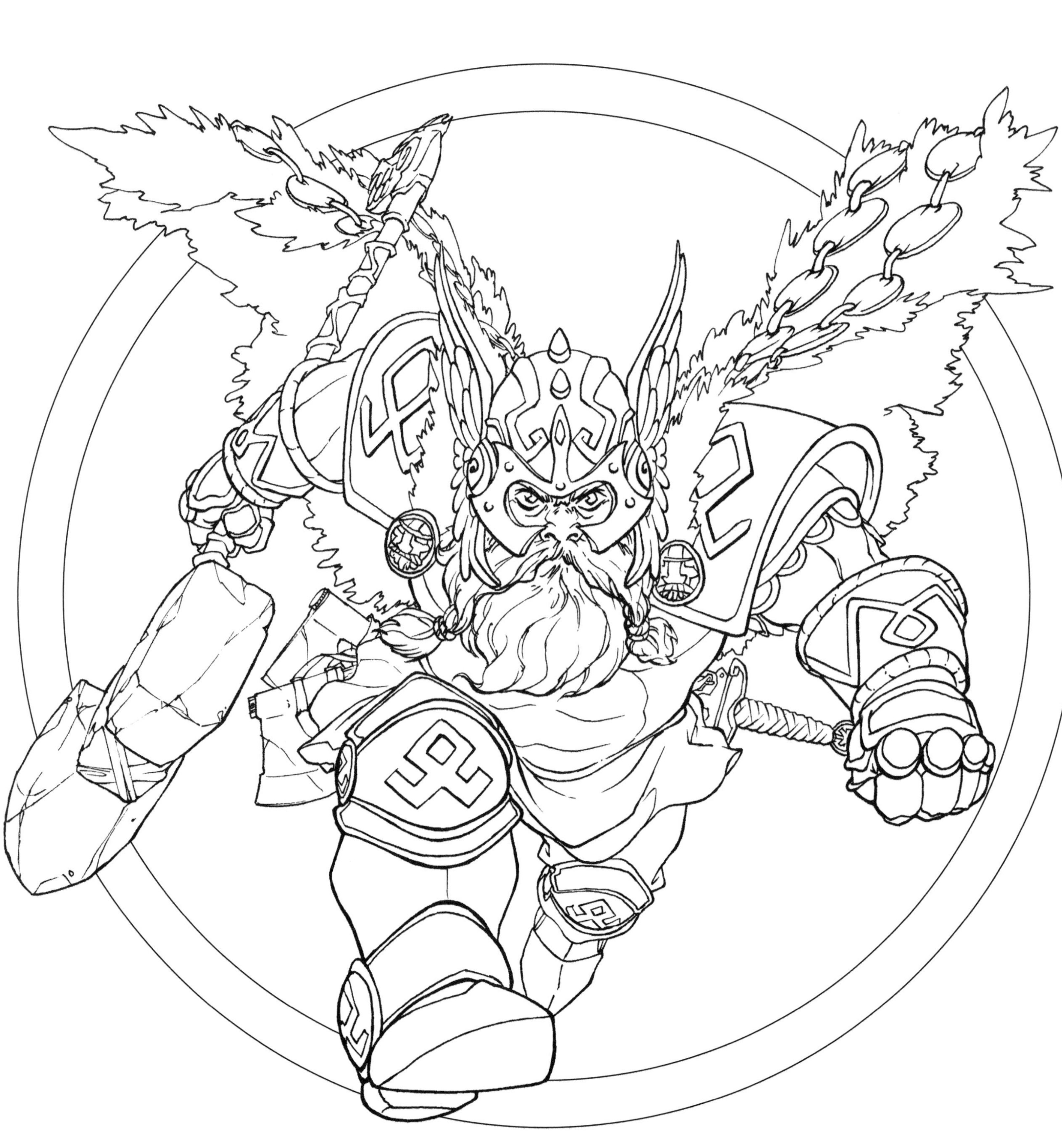

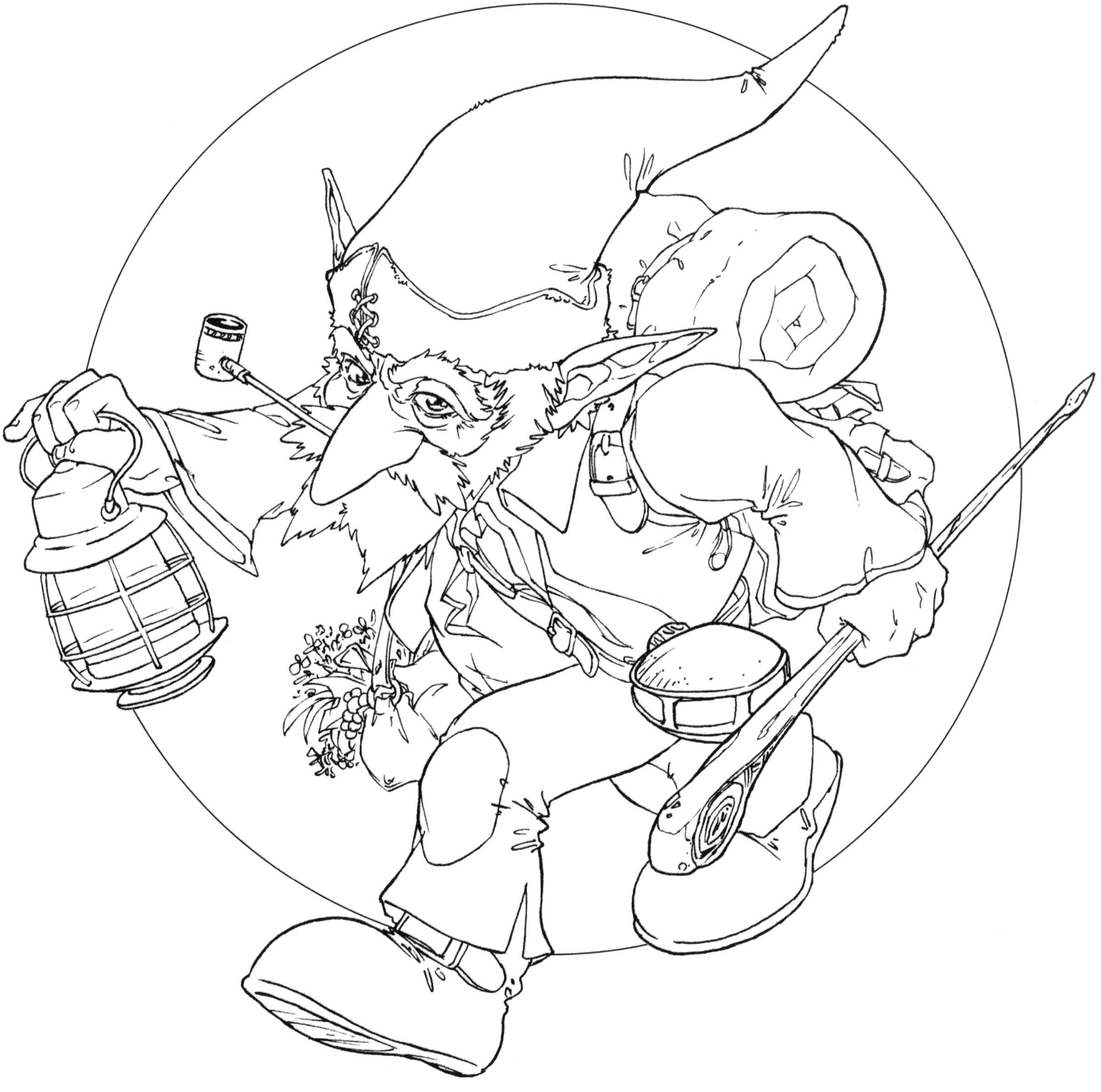

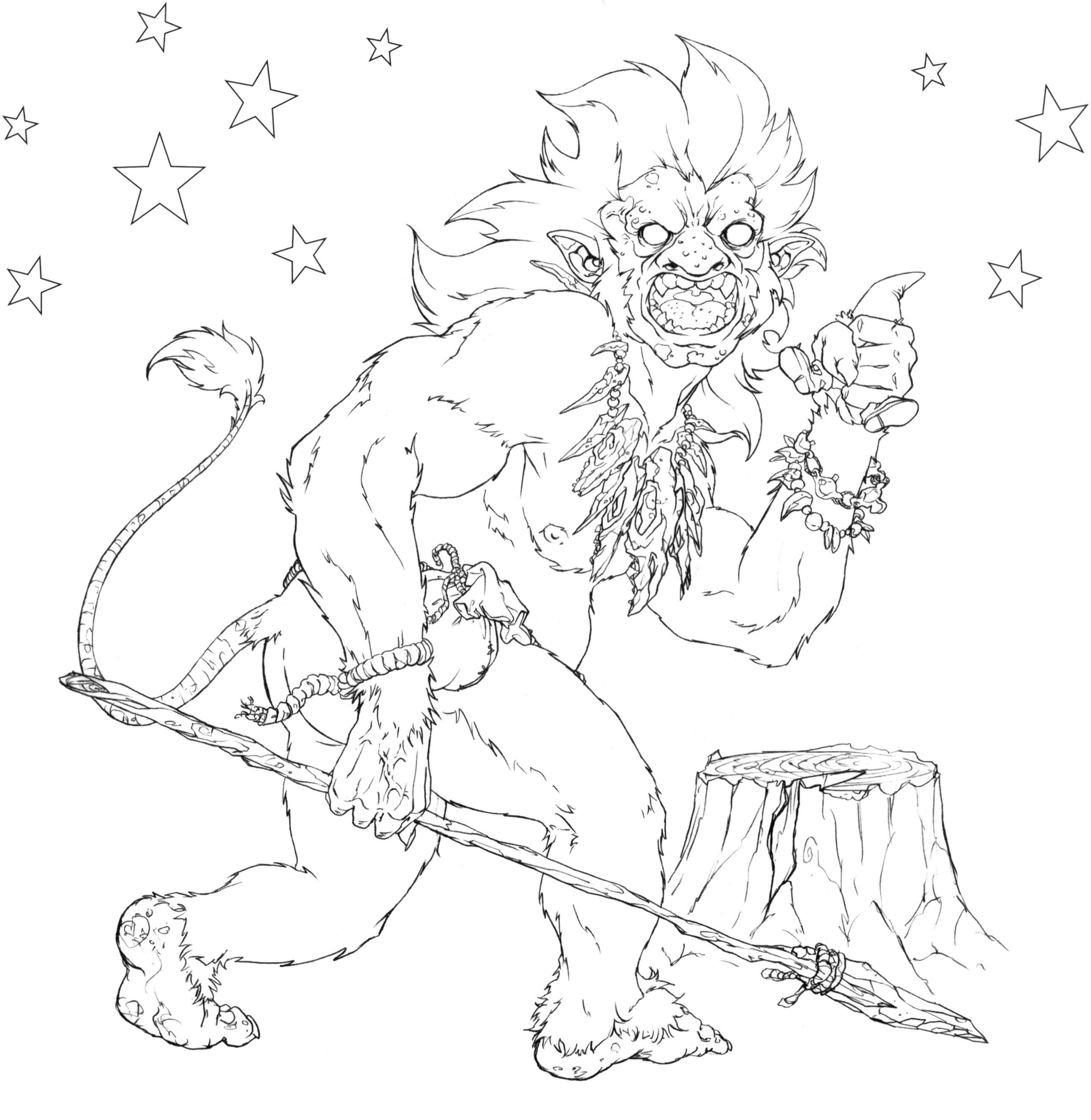

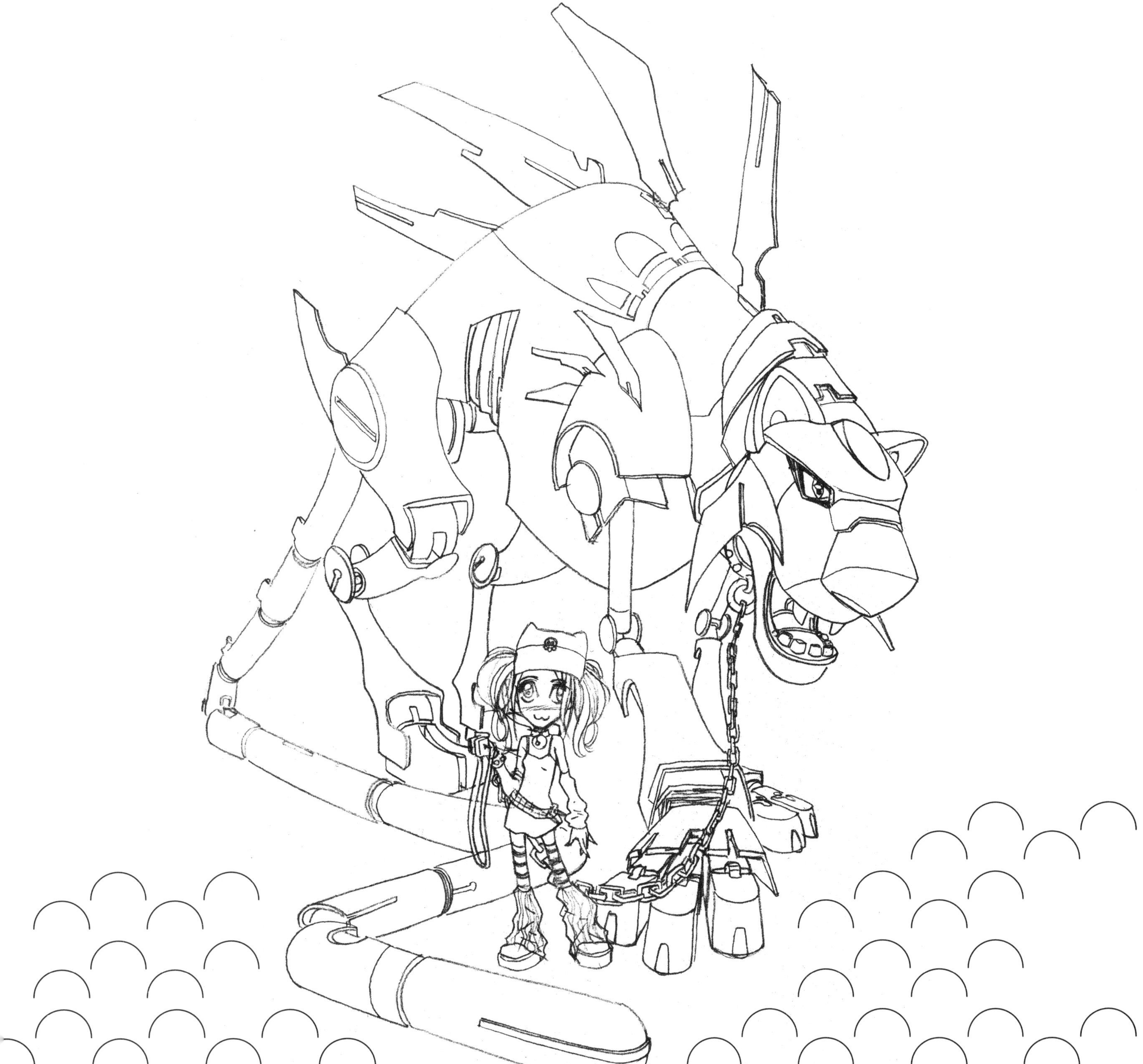

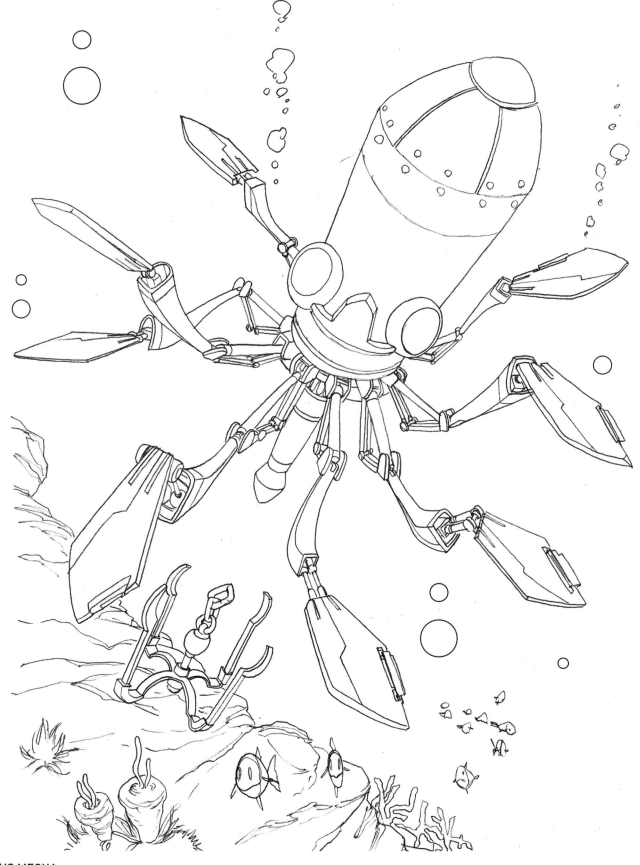

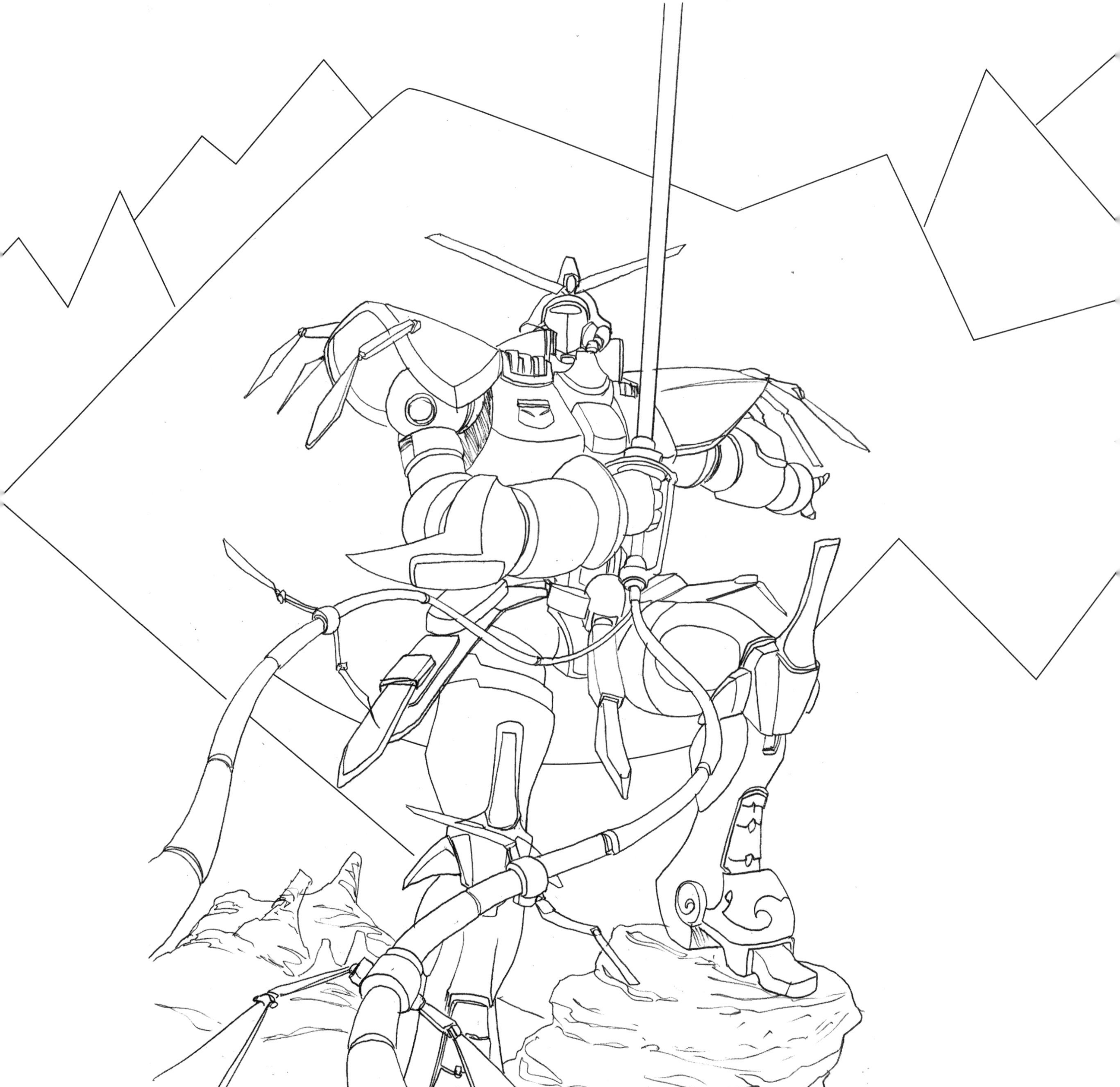

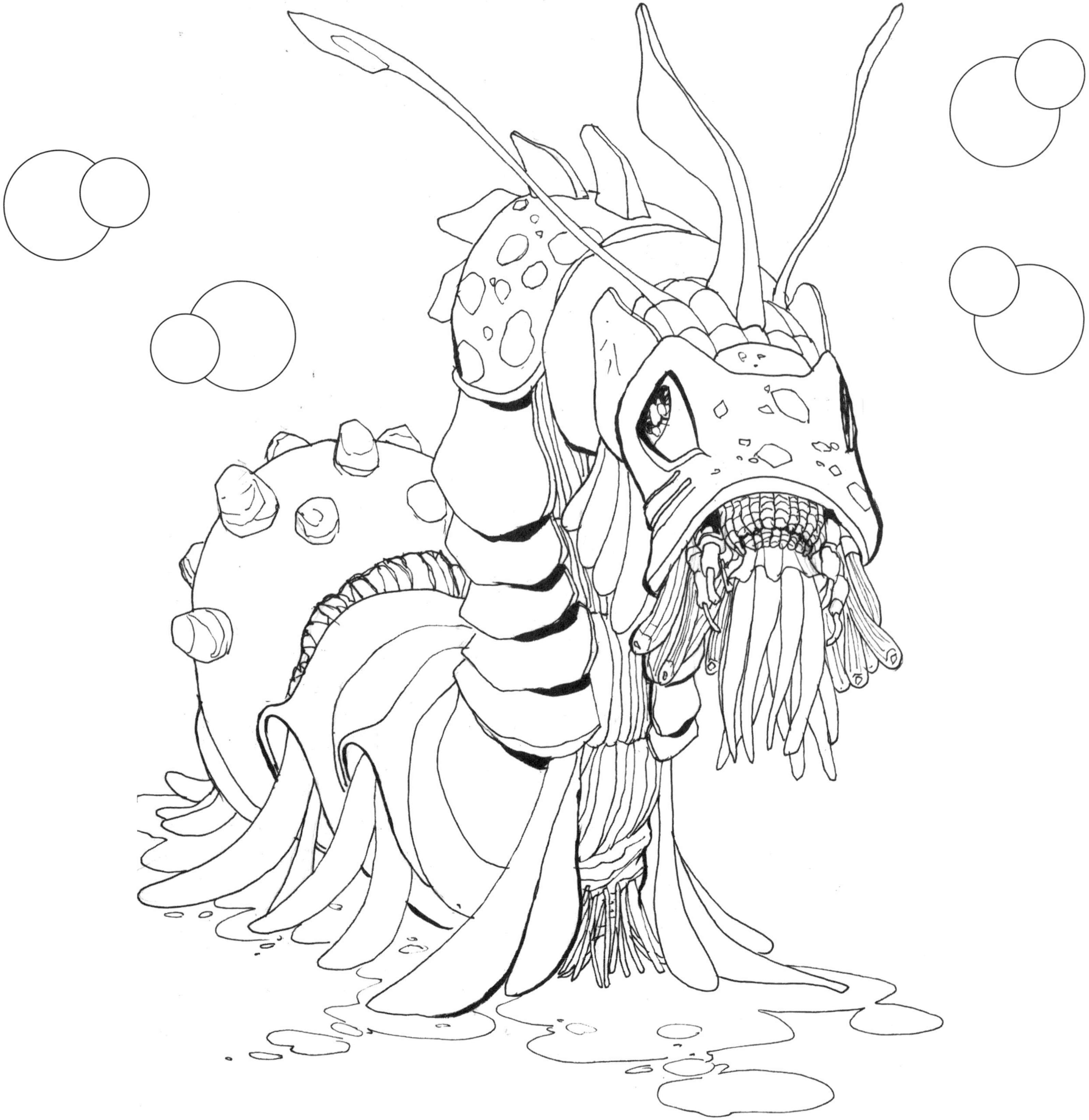

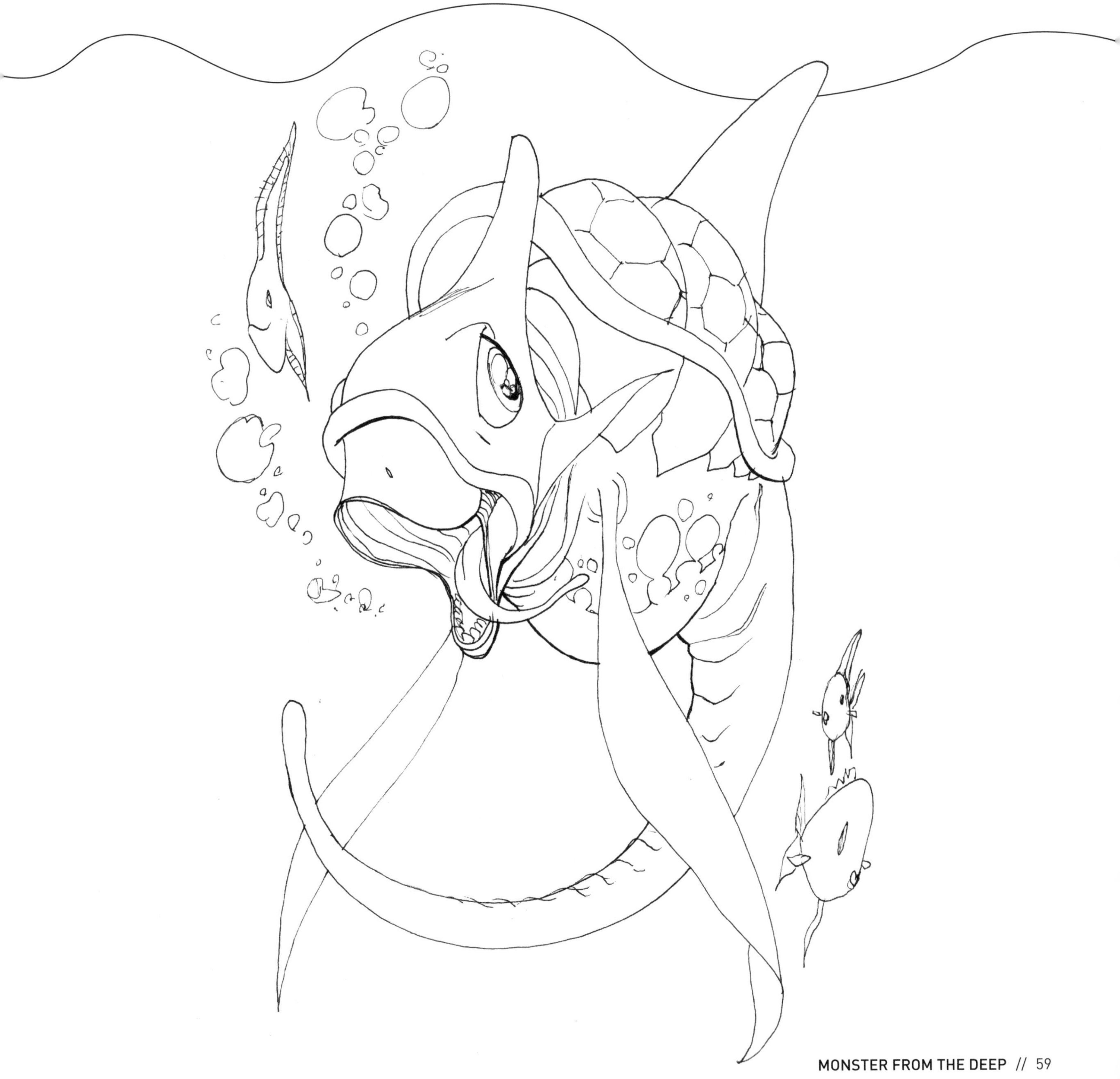

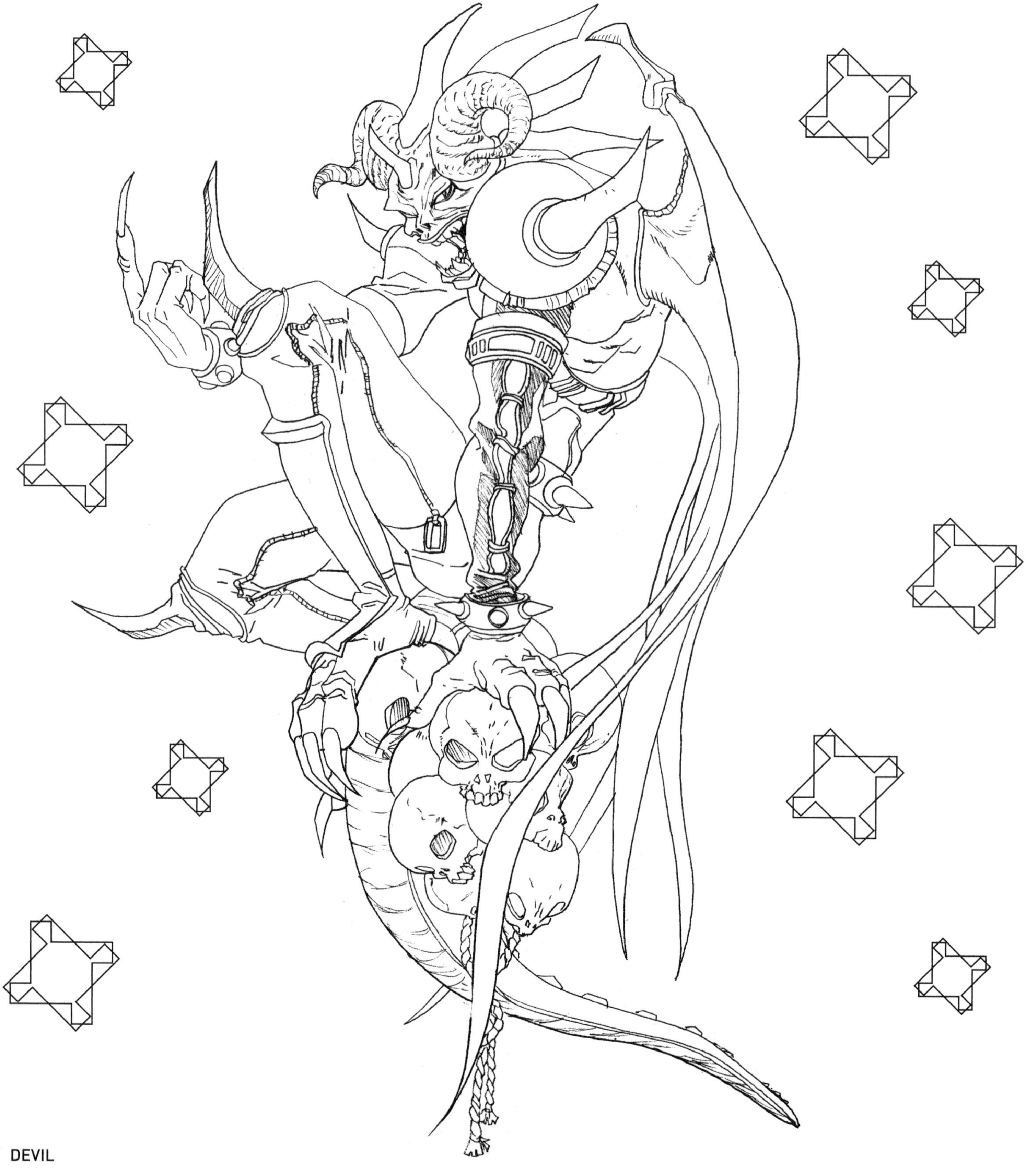

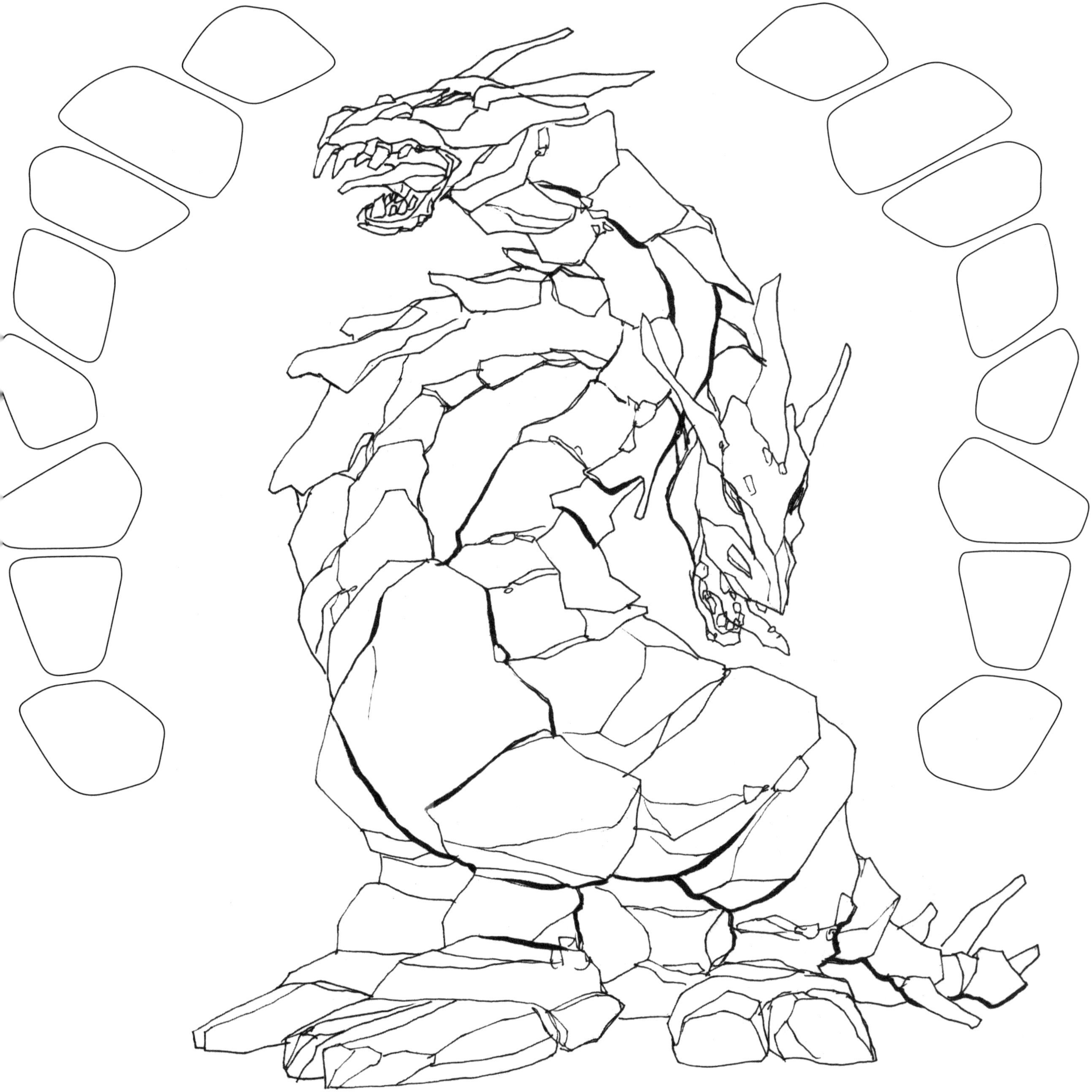

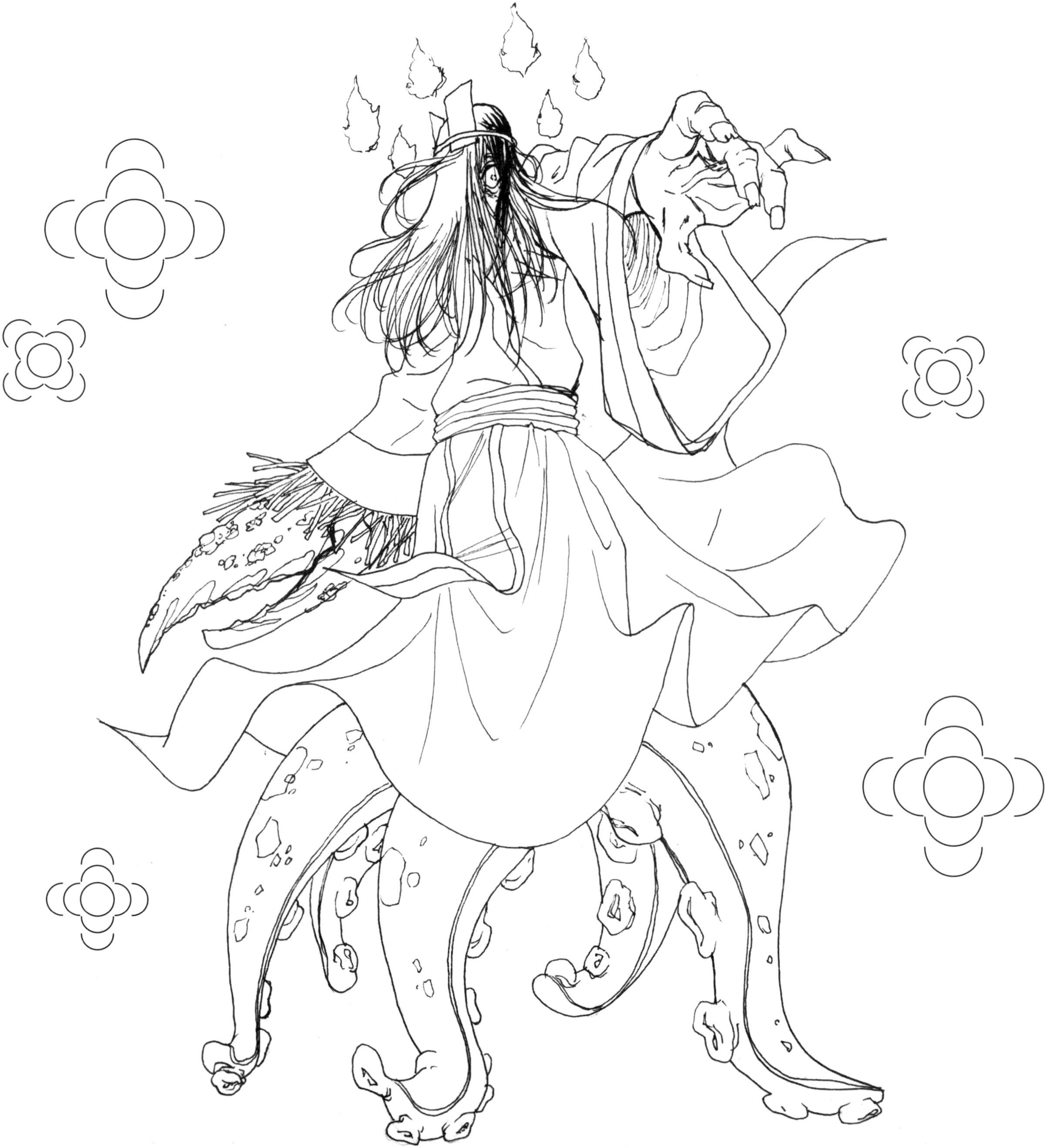

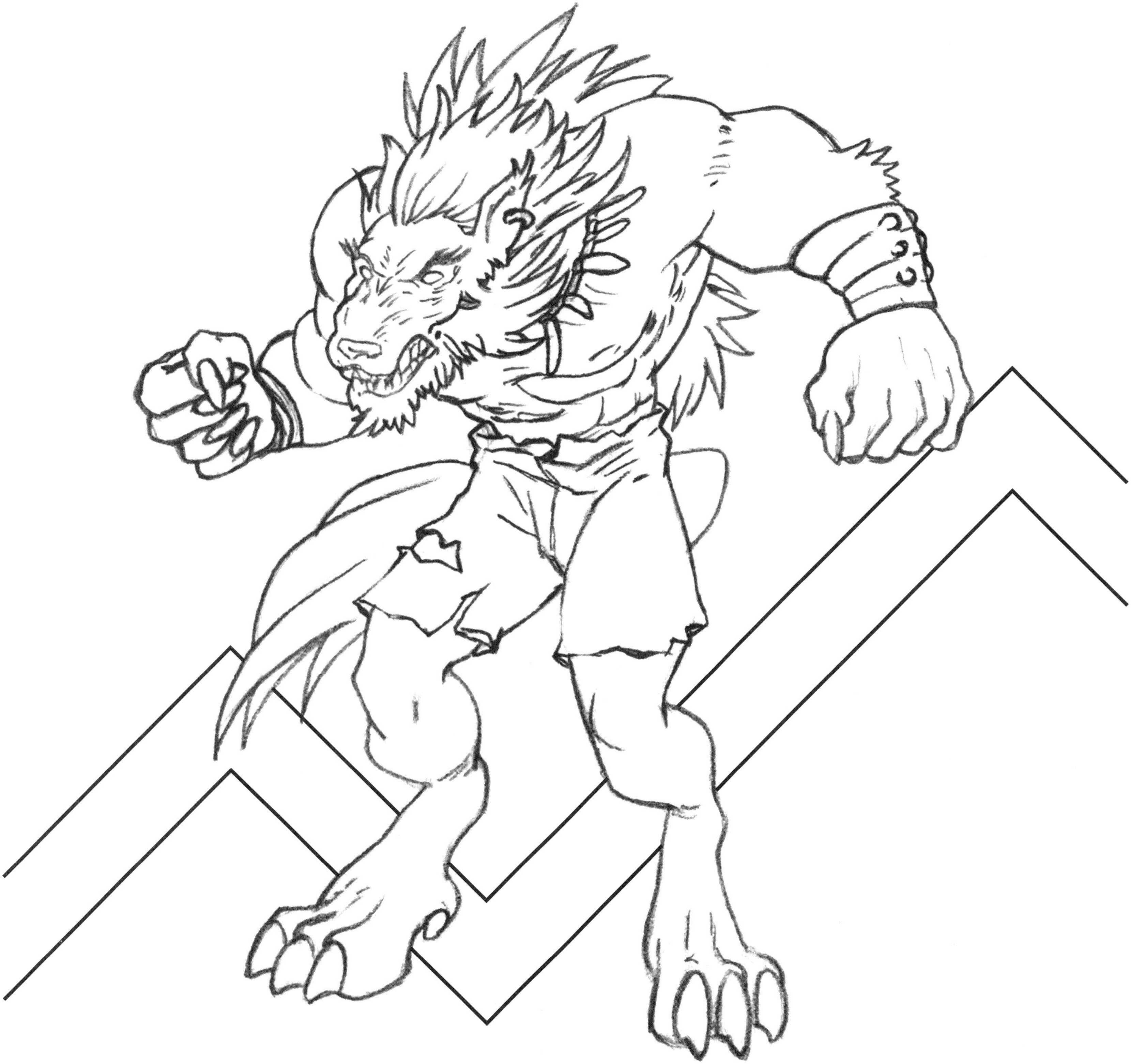

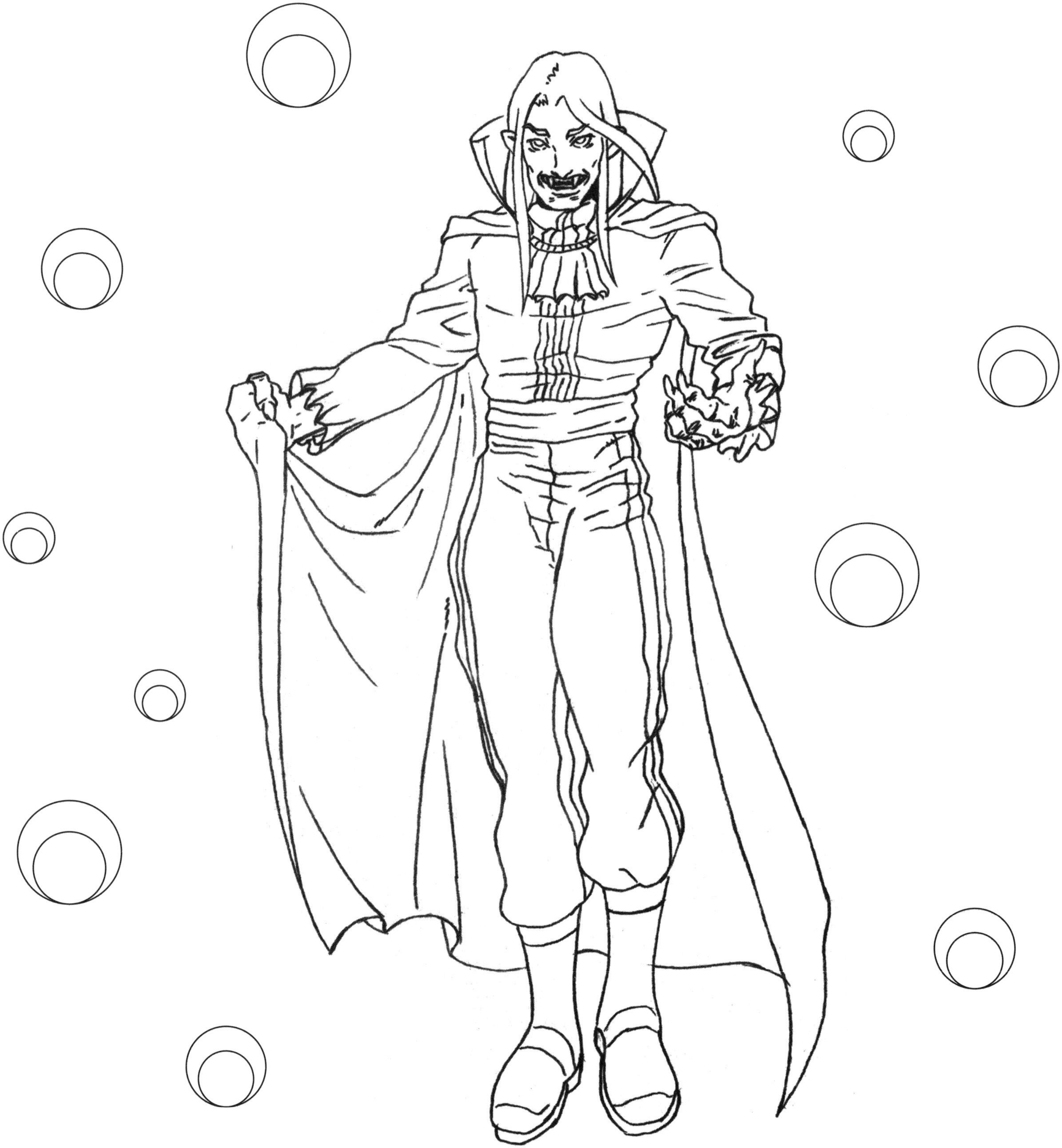

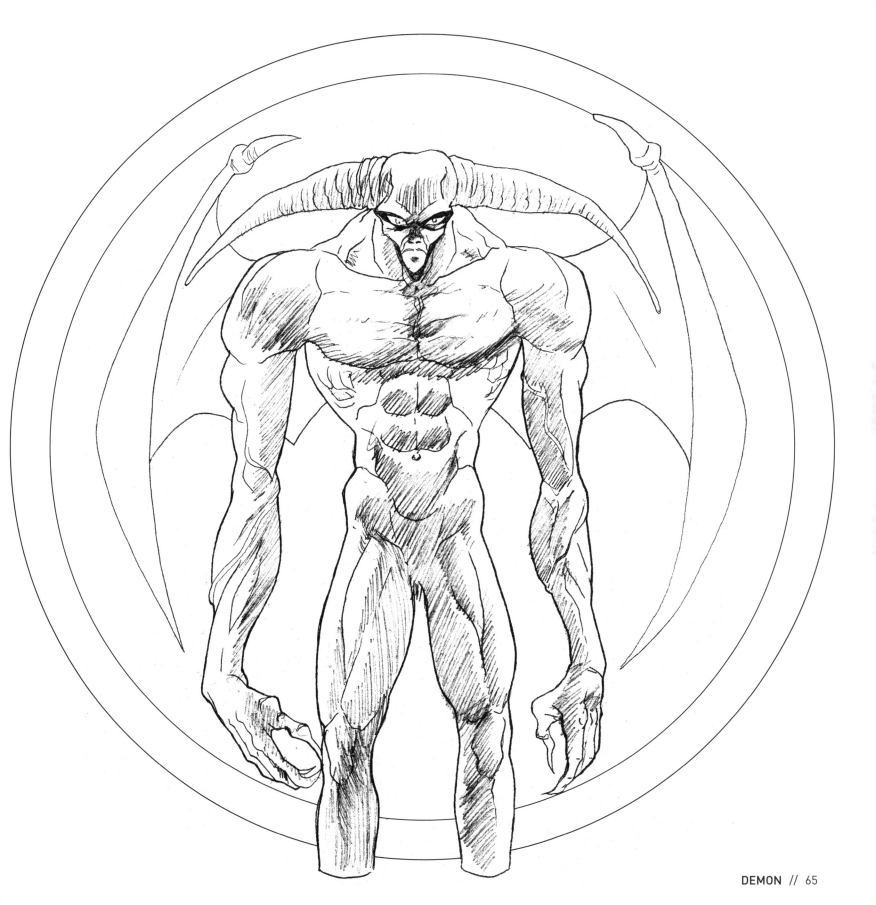

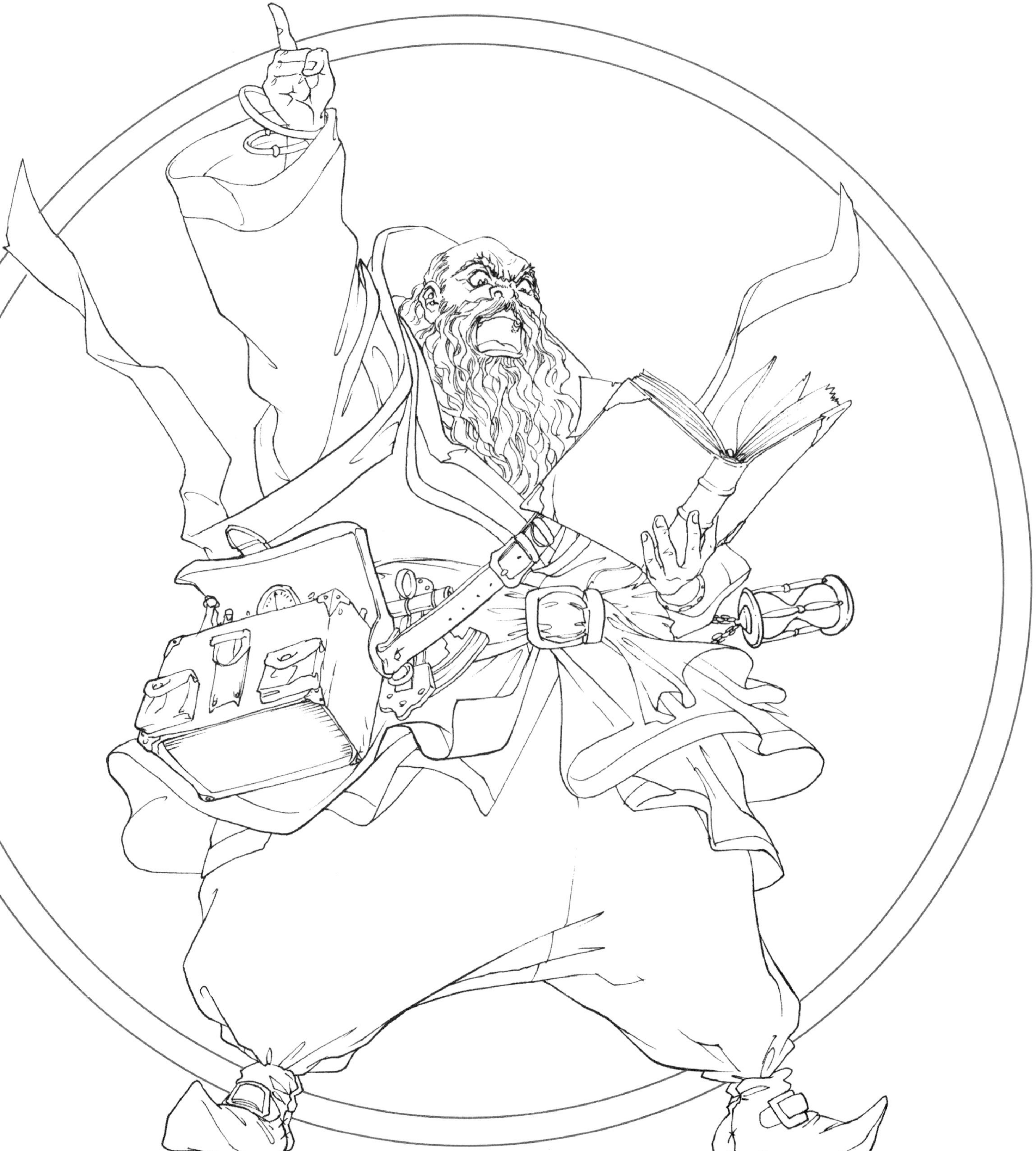

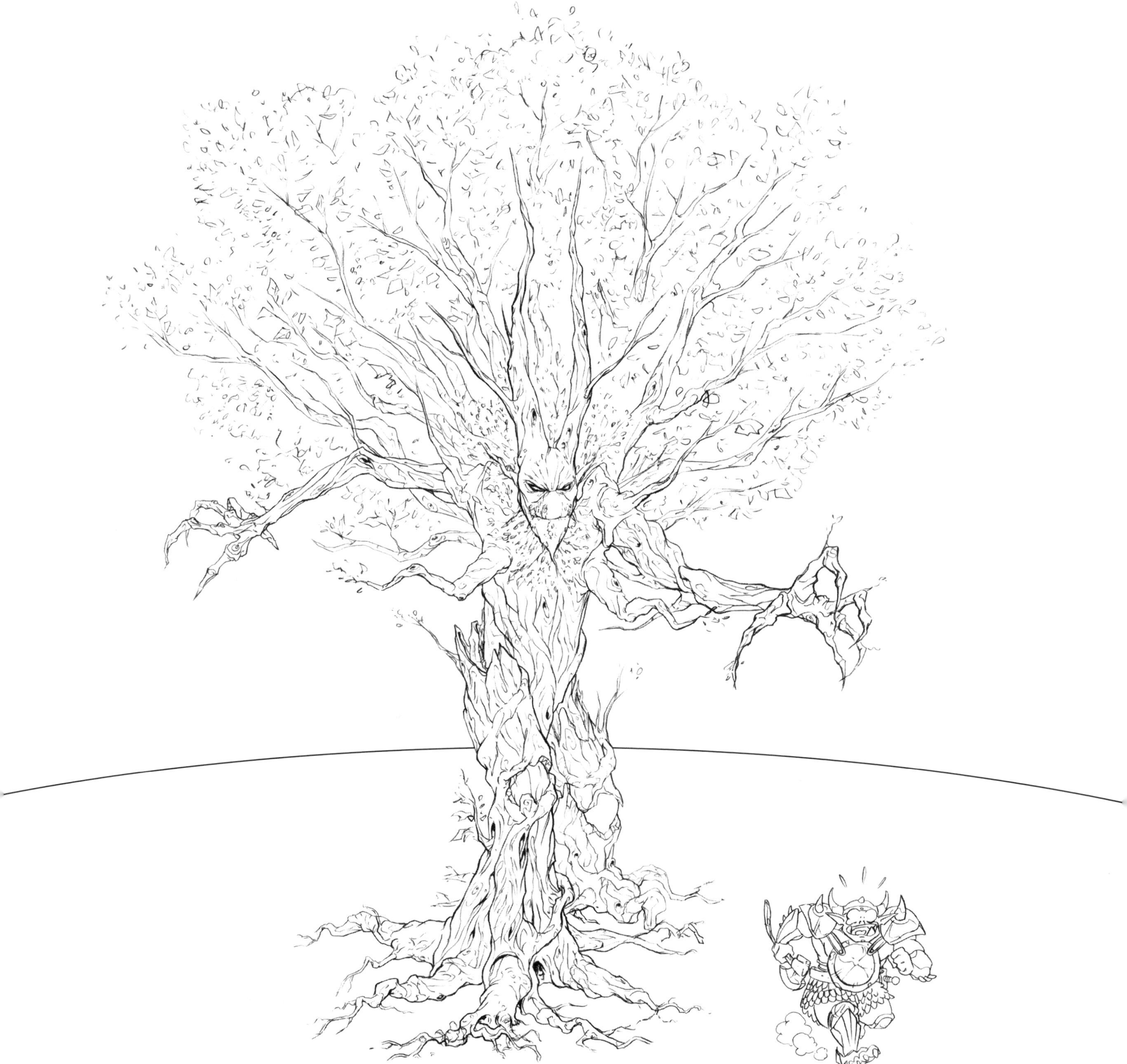

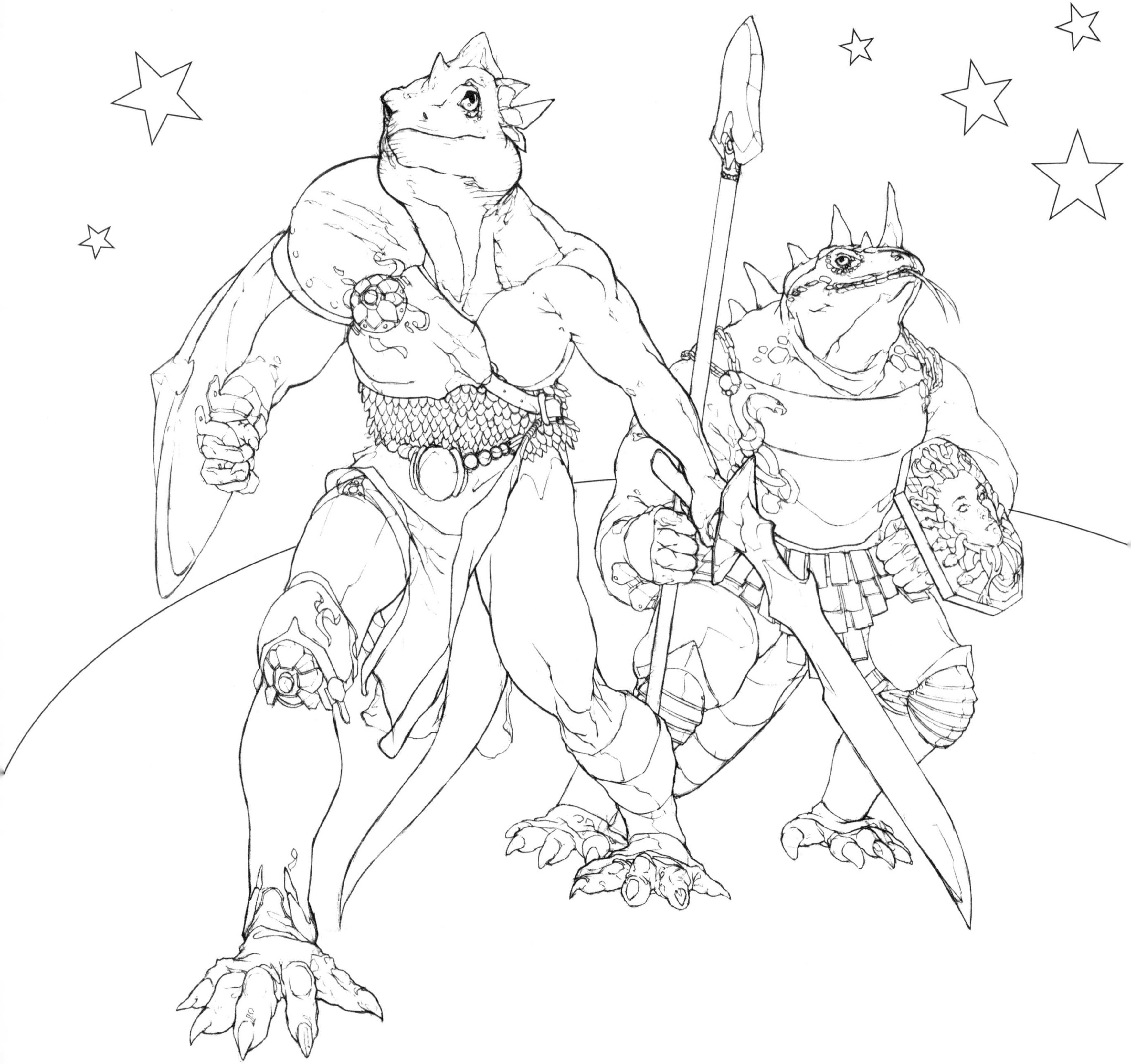

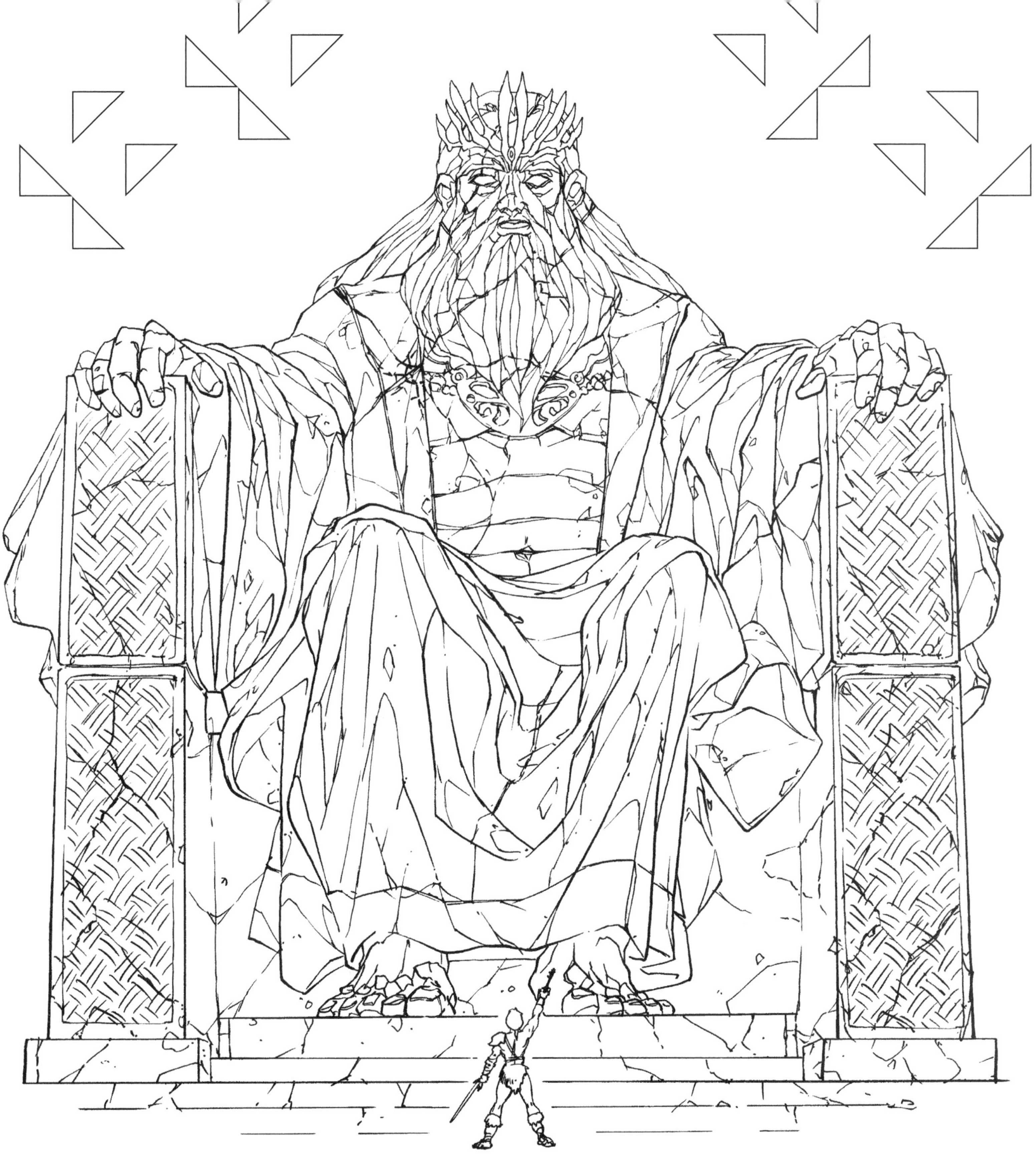

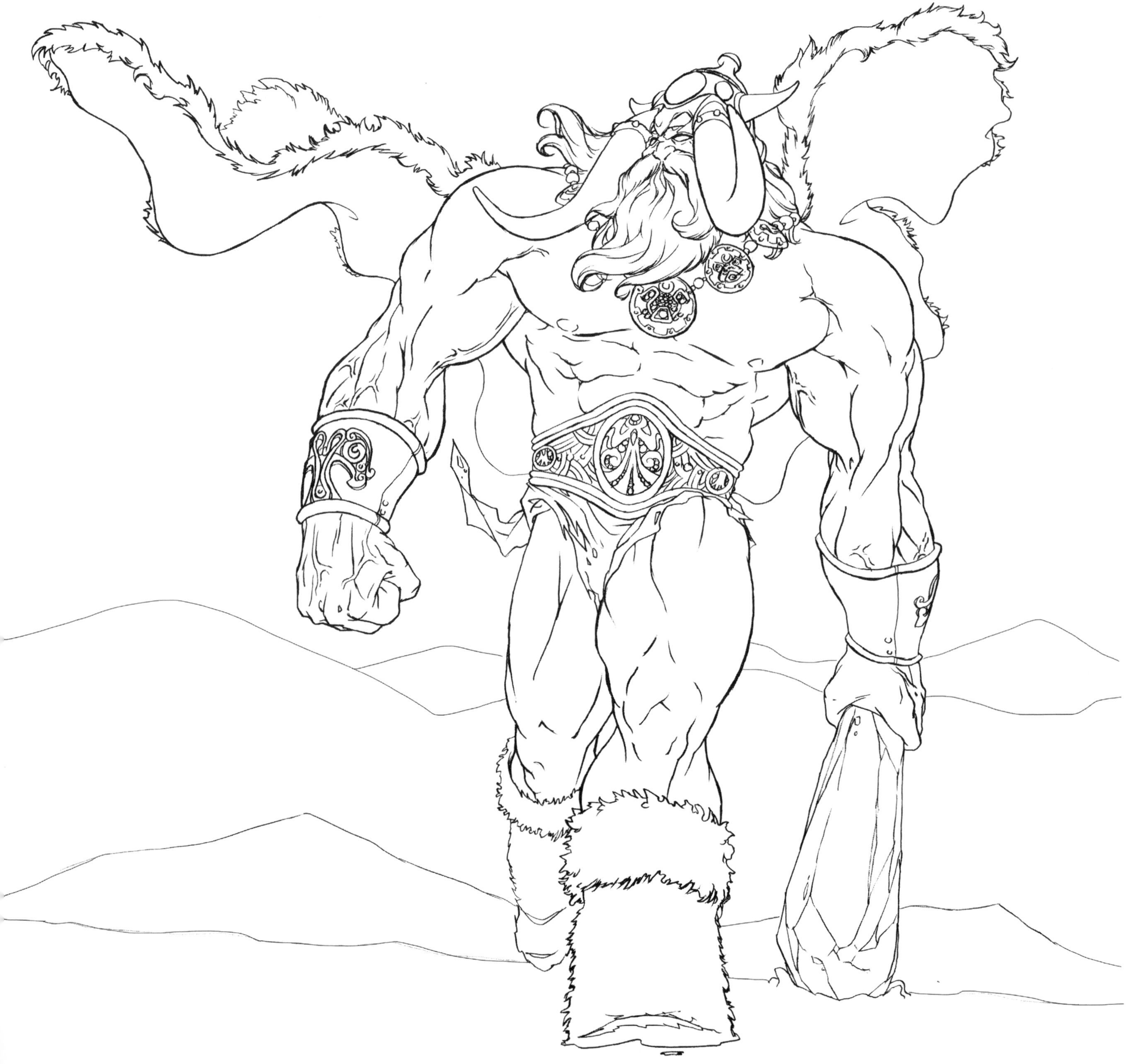

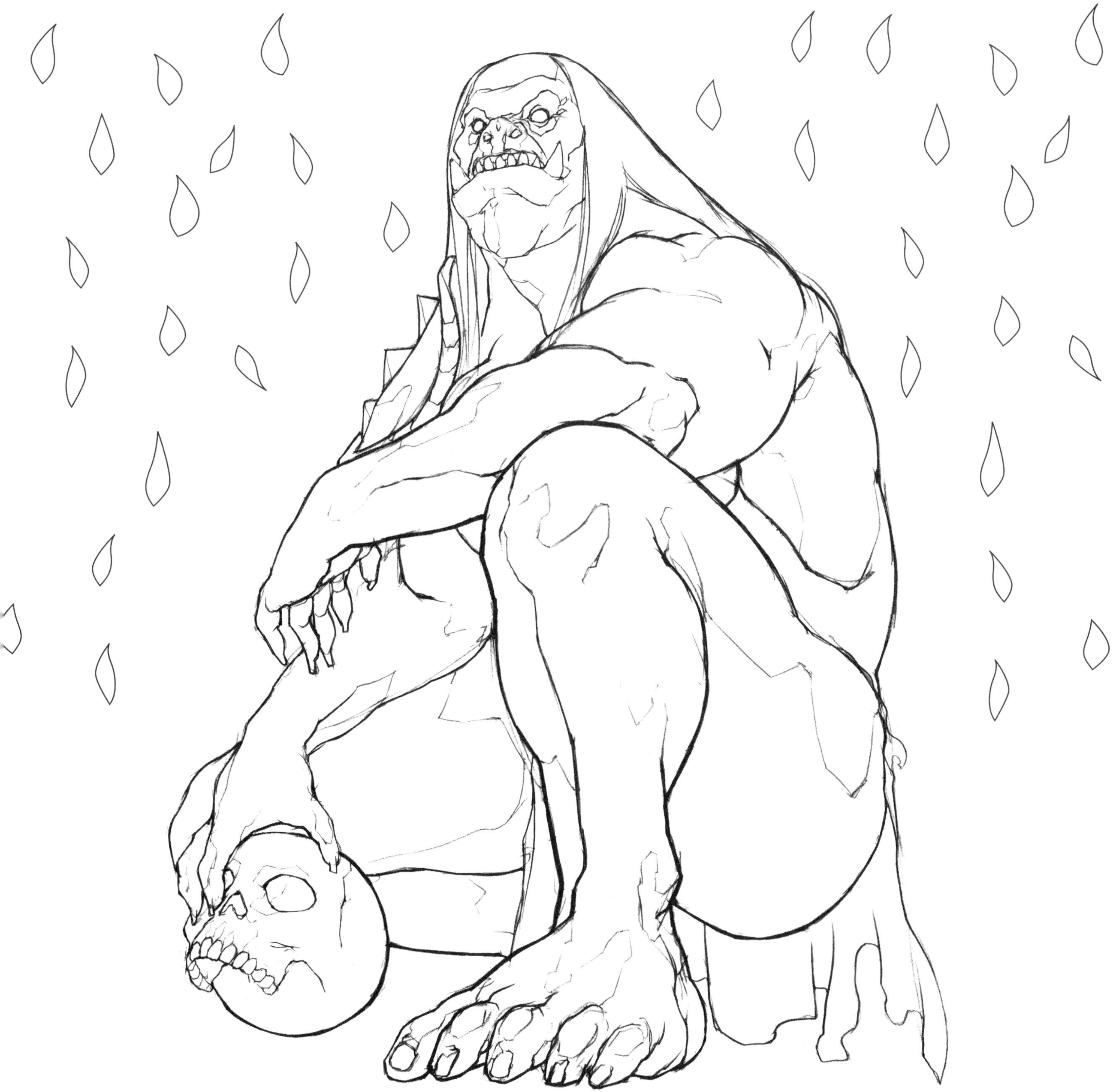

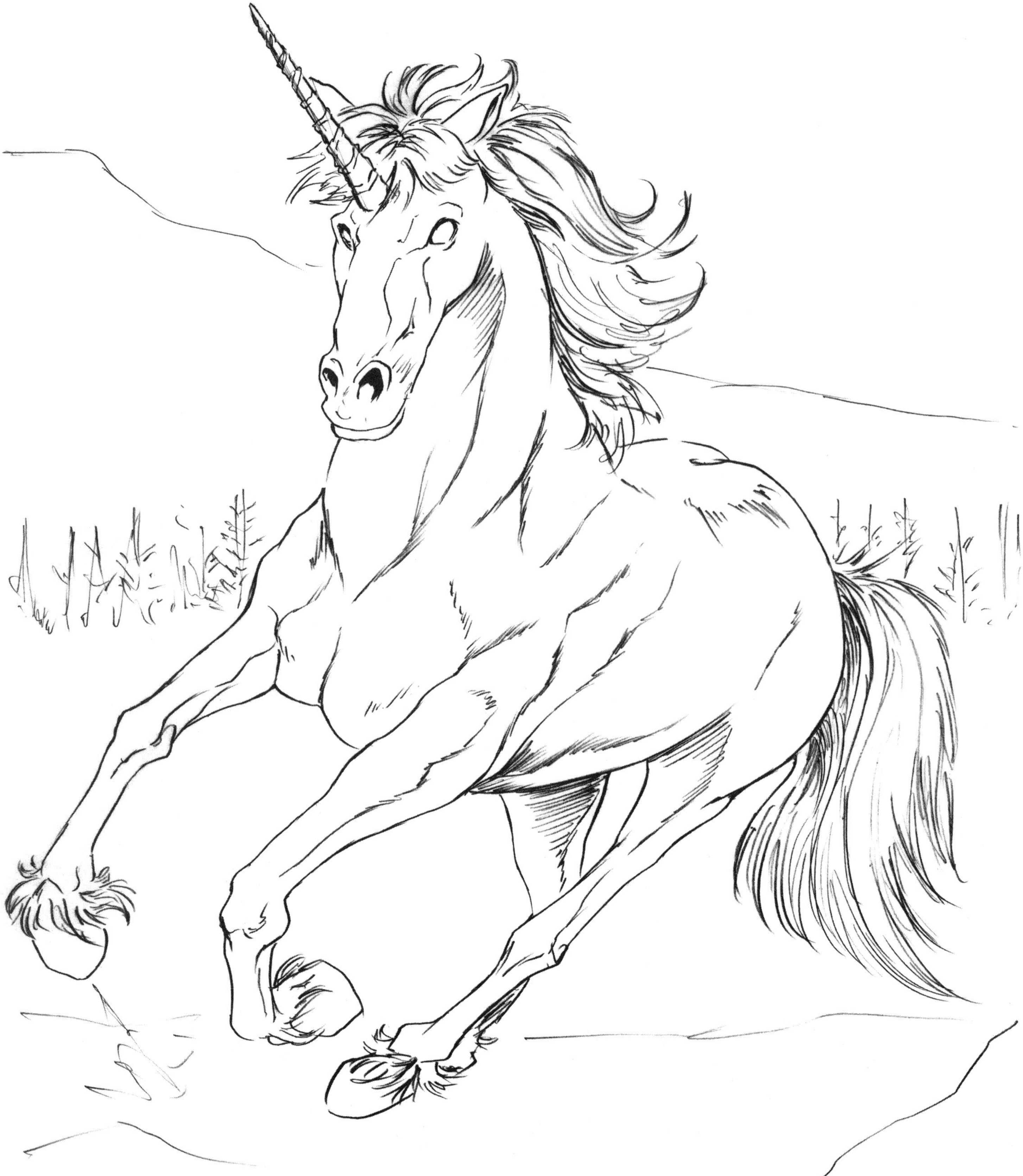

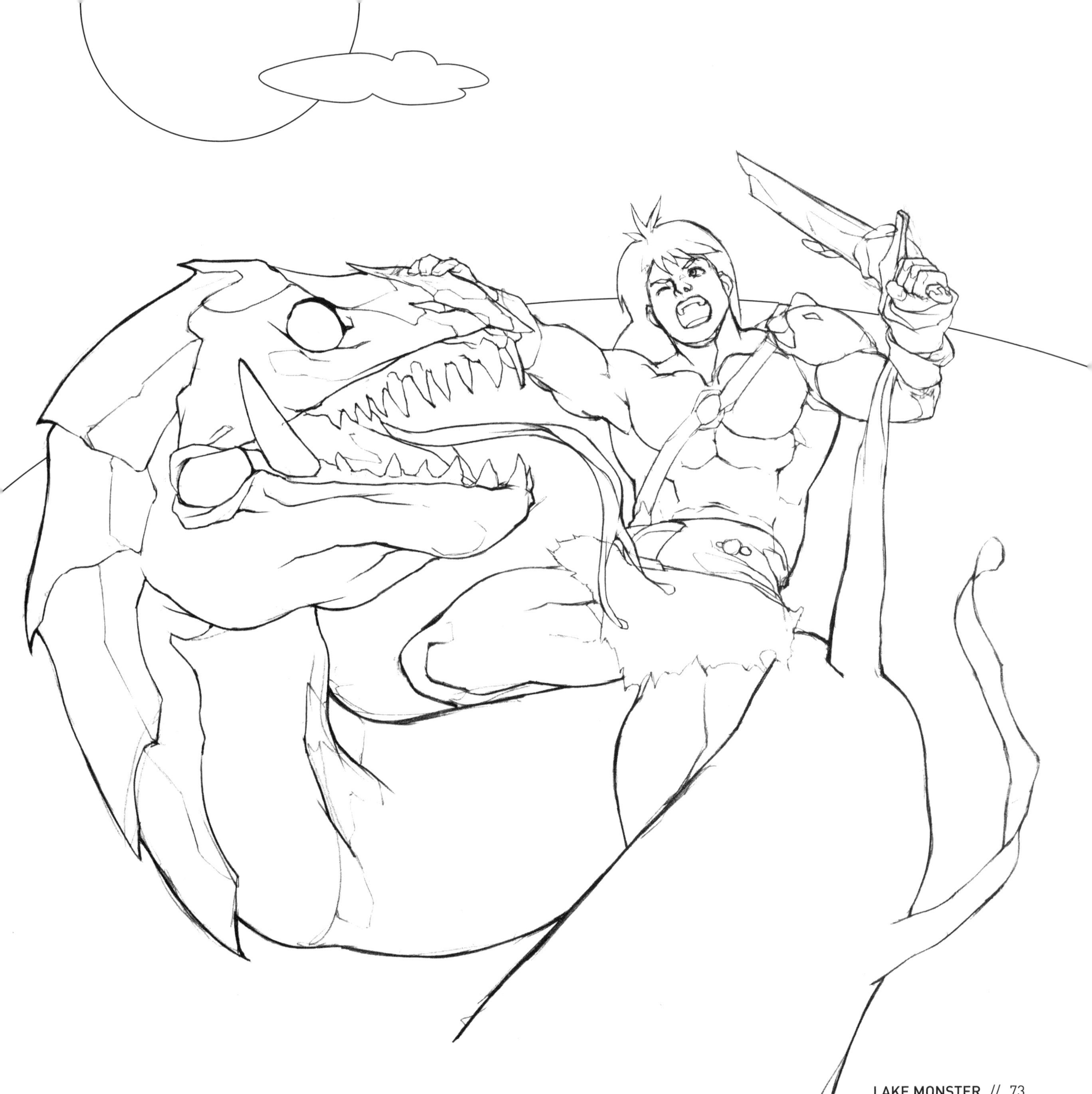

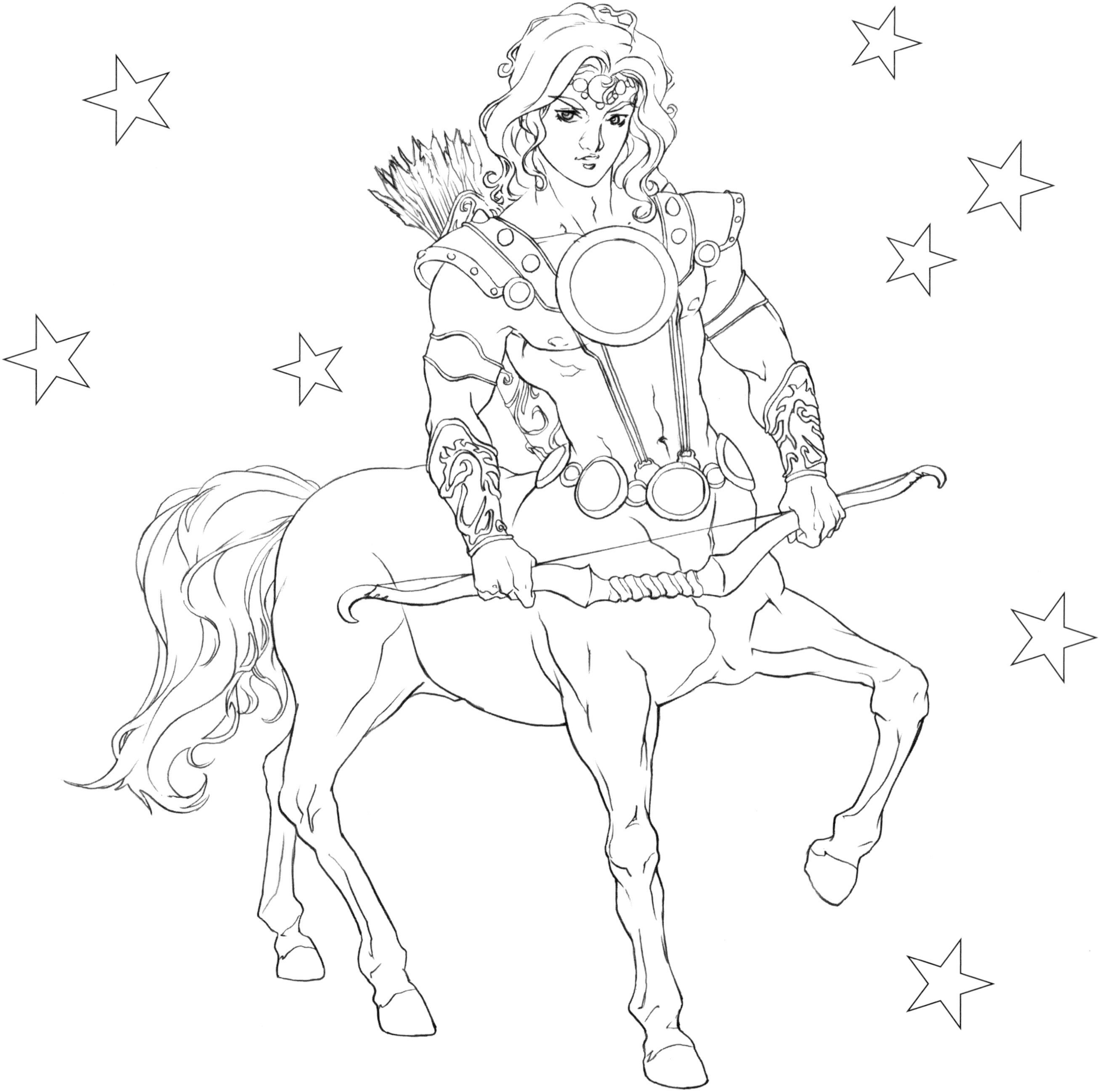

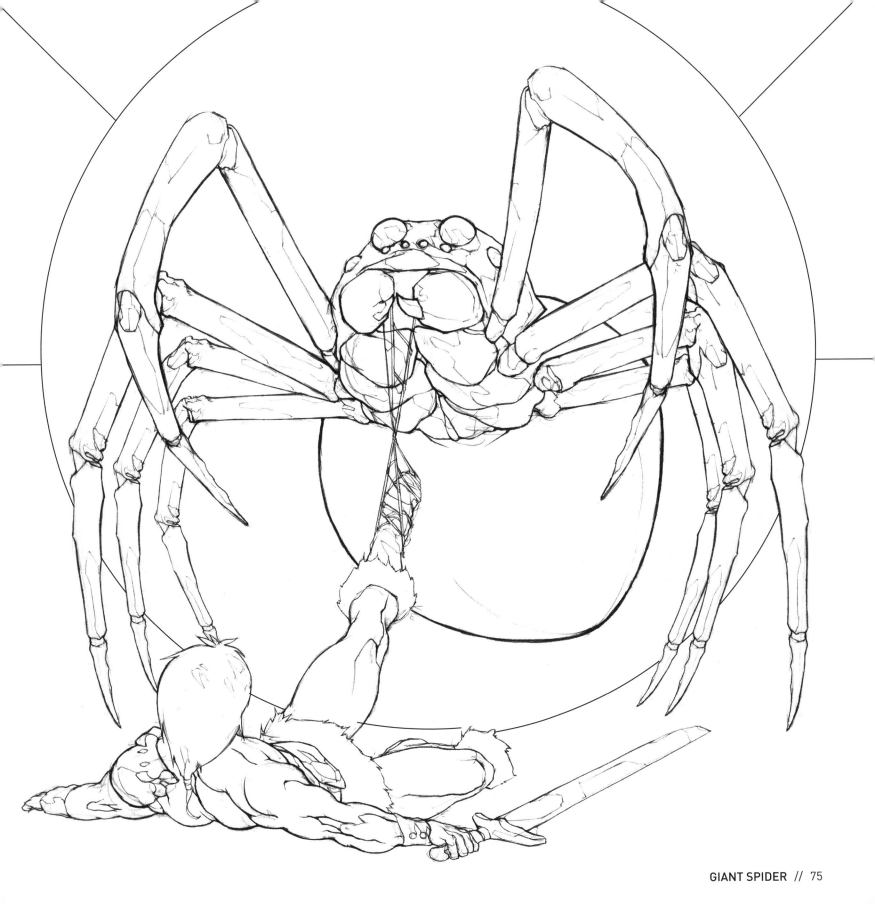

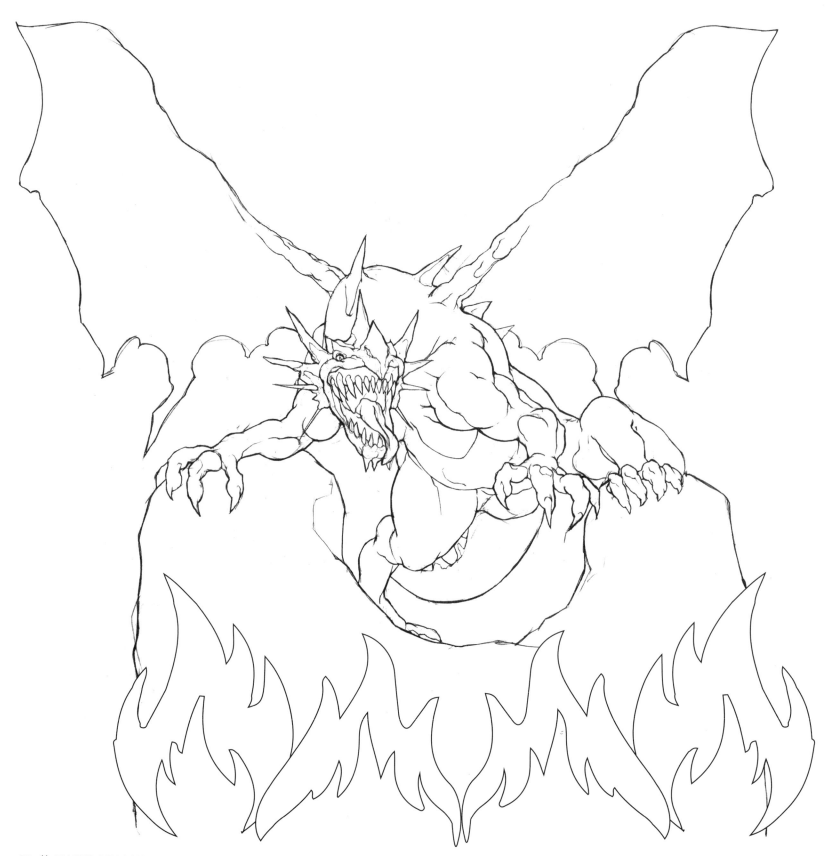

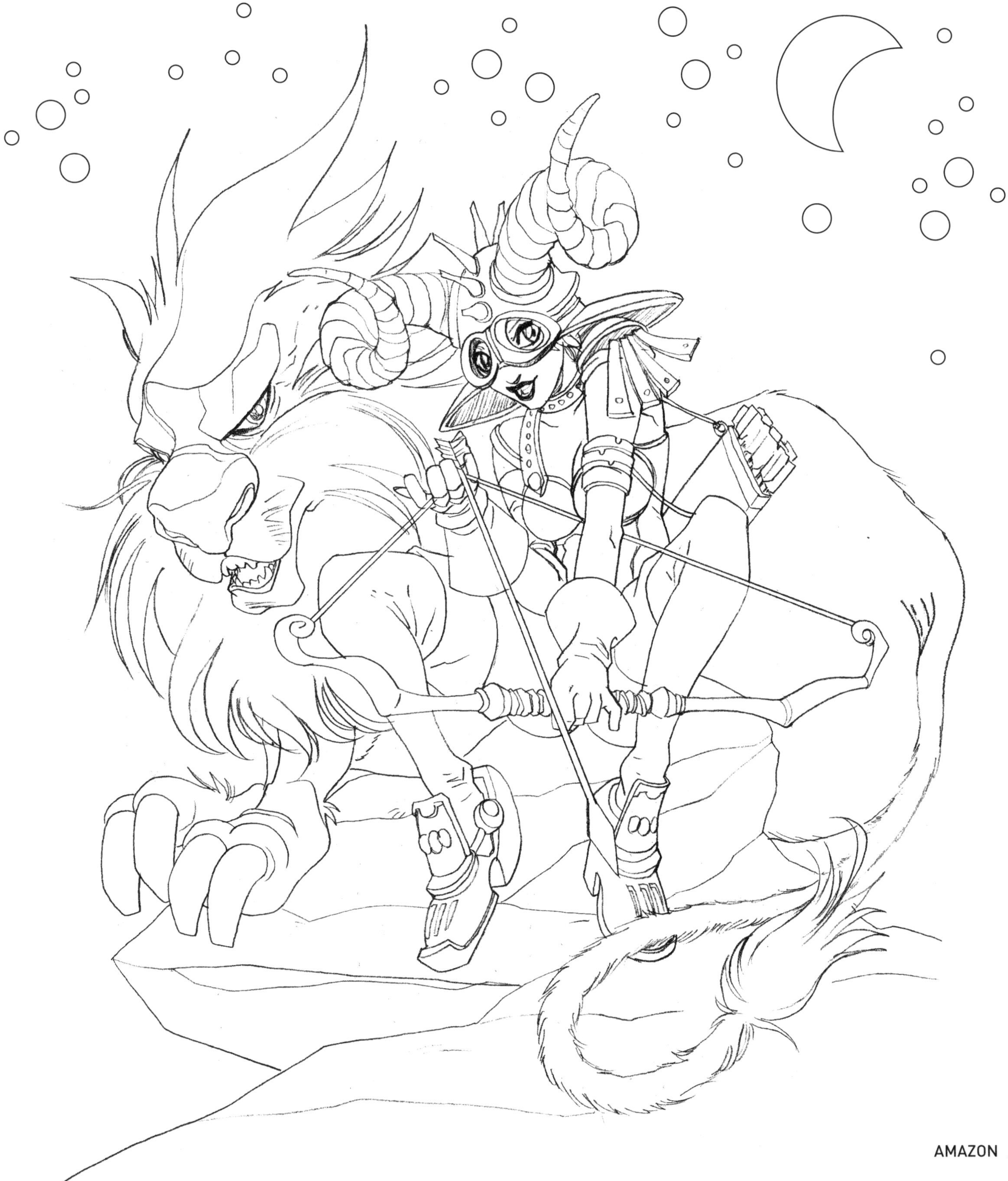

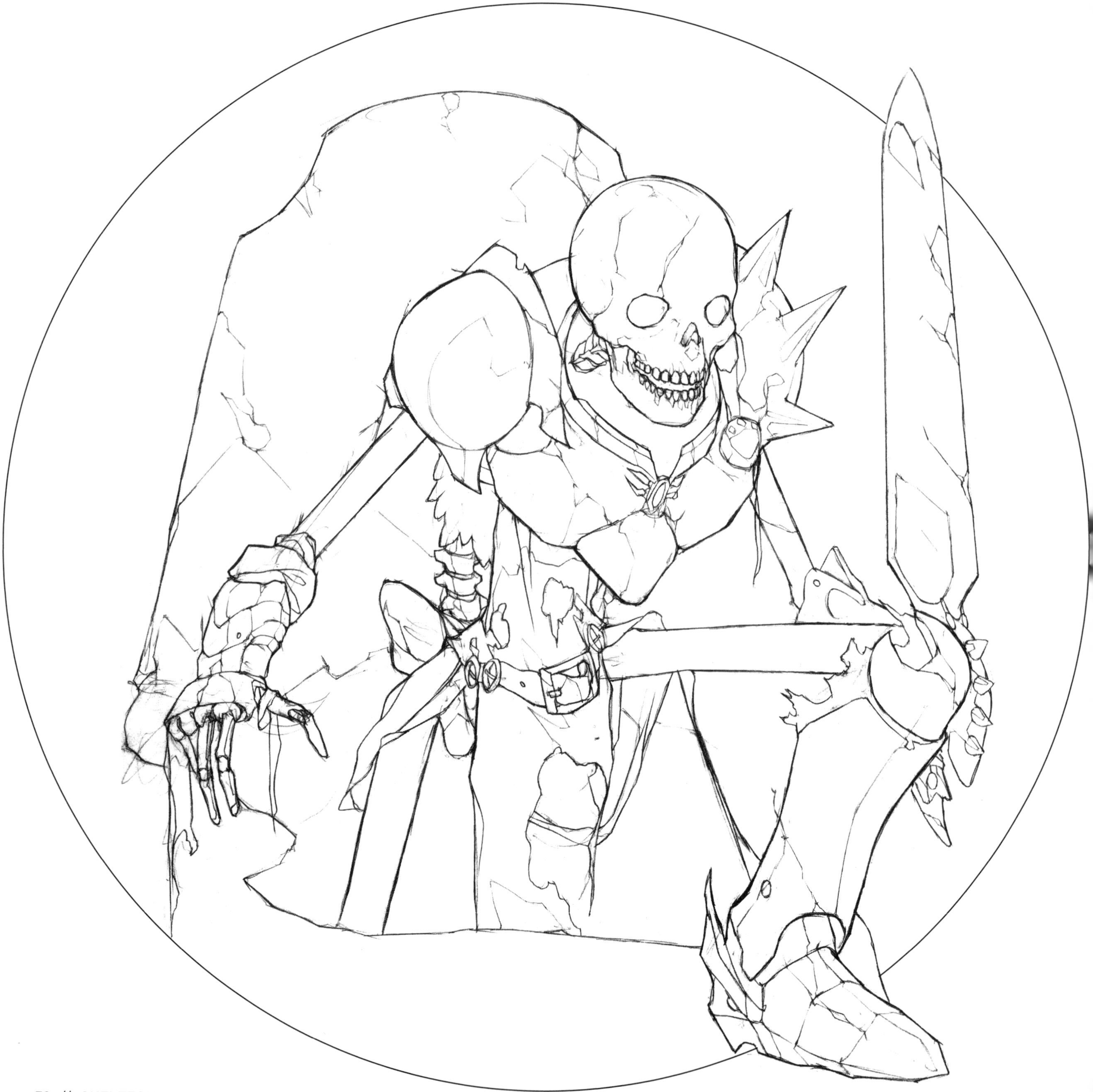

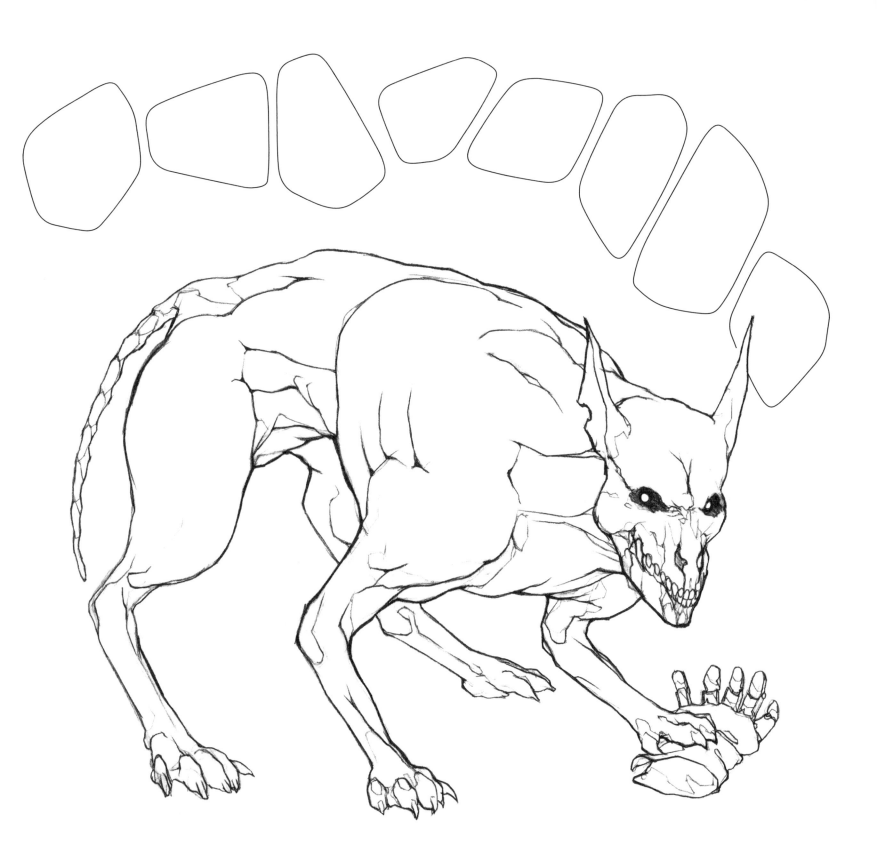

THE MONSTER BOOK OF MANGA CREATURES AND CHARACTERS COLORING BOOK

For information, address Harper Design, 195 Broadway, New York, NY 10007.

HarperCollins books may be purchased for educational, business, or sales promotional use. For information, please email the Special Markets Department at SPsales@harpercollins.com.

First published in 2023 by
Harper Design
An Imprint of HarperCollins*Publishers*
195 Broadway
New York, NY 10007
Tel.: (212) 207-7000
Fax: (855) 746-6023
harperdesign@harpercollins.com
www.hc.com

Distributed throughout the world by
HarperCollinsPublishers
195 Broadway
New York, NY 10007

Editorial coordinator: Claudia Martínez Alonso
Art director: Mireia Casanovas Soley
Illustrations: Estudio Joso and Ikari Studio

ISBN 978-0-06-330606-6

Printed in China